DINOSAUR
· CAKES ·

JACQUI HINE

MEREHURST

A standard spoon measurement is used in all recipes.
1 teaspoon = 5ml spoon
1 tablespoon = 15ml spoon
All spoon measures are level.

Eggs used in the recipes are standard (size 3) unless otherwise stated.

Quantities are given in metric, imperial and cups. Follow one set of measures only as they are not interchangeable.

Published 1991 by Merehurst Limited
Ferry House
51–57 Lacy Road
Putney
London SW15 1PR

© Marshall Cavendish Ltd, 1991

A catalogue record for this book is available from the British Library.

ISBN 1-85391-177-1

Edited by Julia Canning
Designed by Julie Staniland
Photography by Gus Filgate
Illustrations by Simon Roulston
Production by Inger Faulkner
Typeset by MS Filmsetting Ltd, Frome, Somerset

Colour separation by Scantrans Pte Ltd, Singapore
Printed in Hong Kong

The publishers would like to thank Kathy Gummer for her help in the original cake design.

CONTENTS

INTRODUCTION

Dinosaurs and prehistoric animals fire the imagination of everyone both young and old, so what could be more thrilling than a birthday cake in the shape of one of these incredible creatures. Whether you choose a large fierce upright animal or a smaller flat less formidable creature, there's a cake here to suit all ages.

The cakes are easy to make, but some take a little longer to assemble than others. So do read through the recipes first to make sure that you allow yourself enough time to complete the cake. All the cakes can be made in advance (see page 13) and servings are on the generous side.

CAKE-MAKING EQUIPMENT

Most of the equipment needed is readily available from large supermarkets, but specialist cake decorating shops offer a wider choice of cake tins (pans), sugarpaste, food colouring, icing equipment and cakeboards – they even offer a hire service for cake tins.

BAKEWARE

No special cake tins (pans) are required – all the dinosaurs are made from cakes cooked in rectangular and round cake tins (pans) or pudding bowls.

Rectangular tins (pans): use a tin with a base measurement of at least 30 × 20cm/12 × 8in and a depth of 3.5cm/1½in. A roasting tin is ideal for the rectangular sponge and Madeira cakes. A Swiss (jelly) roll tin may be used instead, but it must be lined with a double thickness of greaseproof (waxed) paper to support the sides of the cake.

Use either a roasting tin (pan) or a Swiss (jelly) roll tin for the Swiss (jelly) roll sponge and line the base with non-stick paper.

Round tins (pans): use either a 20cm/8in or 23cm/9in straight-sided sandwich tin as stated in the recipe and line with greaseproof (waxed) paper.

Pudding bowl: use an ovenproof deep bowl and measure its capacity by pouring water from a measuring jug into it. The bowl can be bigger than the capacity stated in the recipe, but if it is too big the cake will be wide at the base and have very little height. Line the base with greaseproof (waxed) paper.

CAKEBOARDS

Large cakeboards, up to 40cm/16in long, can be bought in specialist cake decorating shops, but it is cheaper to make your own – simply cut cardboard boxes down to size and cover with foil. Use several thicknesses of cardboard and make the board at least 7.5cm/3in larger all round than the finished cake size. The length given at the beginning of each recipe indicates the length of the finished cake and is intended as a guide for the size of board required.

Instead of cardboard, you can use plastic-coated shelving for the longer cakes. Alternatively, use planks or trays covered in foil.

THE BASIC CAKES

Each dinosaur recipe states the type of basic cake to use, leaving you with the choice of flavour for the sponge and filling.

Whenever a recipe calls for a rectangular cake always use the sponge recipe unless otherwise indicated.

WHICH CAKE TO CHOOSE

Sponge cake: this is a light, moist cake ideal for stacking and shaping. Use for either flat or upright cakes.

Madeira cake: this has a firmer texture than the sponge cake. Use for single-layered cakes or for making large heads (see page 48).

Swiss roll sponge: this light fatless sponge is best used for rolling up or for covering a rolled shape and is unsuitable for stacking. It could, however, be used as a double-layered cake for the Dinosaur Tableau (see page 68).

Pudding bowl cake: this has a firm texture and should be sliced through horizontally several times and layered with icing. Spread each layer first with warmed sieved jam to make the cake more moist, if desired. Pudding bowl cakes are ideal for hollowing out and filling with sweets or other goodies (see page 79).

Rectangular and round sponge cakes

RECTANGULAR SPONGE CAKE

Ingredients	30 × 20cm/12 × 8in tin (pan)
self-raising flour	250g/8oz/2 cups
baking powder	1 tsp
caster sugar	250g/8oz/1¼ cups
soft margarine	250g/8oz
eggs, beaten	4
hot water	1½ tbsp

Flavourings – add one of the following, if desired:

grated lemon rind	1 lemon
grated orange rind	1 orange
*cocoa powder	45g/1½oz

Substitute cocoa powder for same amount of flour.

To make a fairy bun, see note at end of cake method below.

ROUND SPONGE CAKE

Ingredients	20cm/8in round tin (pan)	23cm/9in round tin (pan)
Self-raising flour	125g/4oz/1 cups	185g/6oz/1½ cup
baking powder	½ tsp	1 tsp
caster sugar	125g/4oz/½ cup	185g/6oz/¾ cup
soft margarine	125g/4oz	185g/6oz
eggs, beaten	2	3
hot water	2 tsp	1 tbsp

Flavourings – add one of the following, if desired:

grated lemon rind	½ lemon	¾ lemon
grated orange rind	½ orange	½ orange
*cocoa powder	22g/¾oz/3tbsp	30g/1oz/¼ cup

Substitute cocoa powder for same amount of flour.

TO MAKE RECTANGULAR AND ROUND SPONGE CAKES

1 Preheat the oven to 190C/375F/Gas 5. Grease and line the base and sides of a 30 × 20 × 3.5cm/ 12 × 8 × 1½in rectangular tin (pan), or the base only of a round tin (see illustrations 1, 2 and 3, page 7). Grease the lining paper.
2 Sift the flour and baking powder (and cocoa powder, if using) into a large bowl.
3 Add the sugar, margarine, beaten eggs and water.

4 Using an electric beater, beat the ingredients together for 1-2 minutes until light and creamy and of a soft dropping consistency. (Alternatively, use a wooden spoon and beat for several minutes.) Add a little more water, if necessary. Stir in the rind, if using.*
5 Place the mixture in the prepared tin, level the surface and spread into the corners of the tin, if necessary.
6 Bake the round cakes for 20–25 minutes and the rectangular cake for 25–30 minutes or until the cake is golden brown and springs back when lightly pressed in the centre.
*To make a fairy bun, remove 1 tablespoon sponge mixture, place in a paper case and bake in the preheated oven for 10 minutes.

TO TURN OUT RECTANGULAR AND ROUND SPONGE CAKES

1 Turn the cake onto a cooling rack and peel off the lining paper. Replace the lining paper and turn the cake over, using a second cooling rack. Leave to cool.
2 When cold, wrap the cake in foil and keep overnight before using.

Rectangular Madeira cake

Ingredients	30 × 20cm/12 × 8in tin (pan)
butter, softened	250g/8oz
caster sugar	250g/8oz/1¼ cups
grated lemon rind	1 lemon
eggs, beaten	4
ground almonds	90g/3oz/¾ cup
self-raising flour, sifted	375g/12oz/3 cups
lemon juice	1 lemon

Flavourings – add one of the following, if desired:

glacé cherries, chopped	125g/4oz/¾ cup
crystalised ginger, chopped	125g/4oz/¾ cup
chocolate chips	90g/3oz/½ cup

Pudding bowl cake

Ingredients	1.25L/ 40fl oz/ 5 cup bowl	1.57L/ 50fl oz/ 6 cup bowl	1.87L/ 60fl oz/ 7 cup bowl
self-raising flour	185g/ 6oz/1½ cups	250g/ 8oz/2 cups	315g/ 10oz/ 2½ cups
caster sugar	185g/ 6oz/¾ cup	250g/ 8oz/1¼ cups	315g/ 10oz/ 1½ cups
soft margarine	185g/ 6oz	250g/ 8oz	315g/ 10oz
eggs, beaten	3	4	5
hot water	1 tbsp	1½ tbsp	2 tbsp

Flavourings – add one of the following, if desired:

grated lemon rind	1 lemon	1 lemon	1½ lemons
grated orange rind	1 orange	1 orange	1½ oranges
*cocoa powder	30g/1oz/ ¼ cup	45g/1½oz/ ⅓ cup	60g/2oz/ ½ cup

* Substitute for same amount of flour

TO MAKE A RECTANGULAR MADEIRA CAKE

1 Preheat the oven to 180C/350F/Gas 4. Grease and line a 30 × 20 × 3.5cm/12 × 8 × 1½in rectangular tin (pan) (see illustrations 1 and 2, page 7). Grease the lining paper.

2 Cream the butter, sugar and lemon rind in a bowl until light and fluffy. Beat in the eggs a little at a time.

3 Mix the ground almonds and chosen flavouring together in another bowl. Fold into the creamed mixture, alternating with the flour, until well mixed. Add the lemon juice to make a soft consistency.

4 Place the mixture in the prepared tin, level the surface and spread into the corners.

5 Bake for 50-60 minutes until the cake is golden brown and feels firm to the touch.

6 Leave to cool in the tin for 15 minutes before turning out. Leave the lining paper in place until you are ready to cut. Wrap the cake in foil and store for several days if wished.

TO MAKE A PUDDING BOWL CAKE

1 Preheat the oven to 180C/350F/Gas 4. Grease and line the base of a pudding bowl (see illustration 3, page 7). Grease the paper, then stand the bowl on a baking tray.

2 Sift the flour (and cocoa powder, if using) into a large bowl.

3 Add the sugar, margarine, eggs and water.

4 Using an electric beater, beat the ingredients together for 1-2 minutes until the mixture is light and creamy and of a soft dropping consistency. (Alternatively, use a wooden spoon and beat for several minutes.) Stir in the lemon or orange rind, if using.

5 Place in the prepared bowl and bake for 20 minutes, then reduce the oven temperature to 160C/325F/Gas 3 and continue to cook for 1-1¼ hours until a fine skewer inserted into the cake comes out clean. Cover with greaseproof (waxed) paper during cooking to prevent the top from overbrowning.

6 Turn out onto a cooling rack and peel off the lining paper. Leave to cool. When cold, wrap in foil and keep overnight before using.

Lining Bakeware

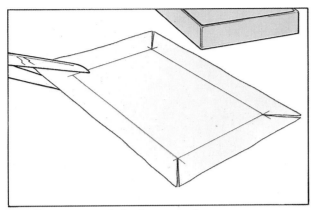

1 Draw round tin base and cut out paper, leaving a 5cm/2in margin. Snip corners.

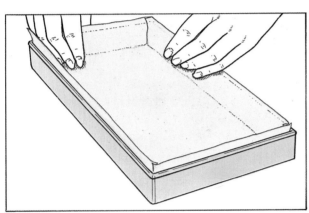

2 Press the paper into the tin, overlapping the corners. The paper stands above sides.

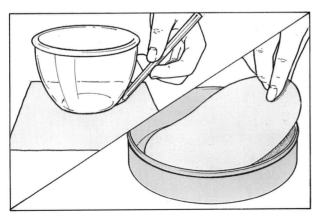

3 Draw round bowl or tin. Cut out the paper and use to line base.

Swiss roll sponge

Ingredients	30 × 20cm/12 × 8in tin (pan)
self-raising flour or plain flour	90g/3oz/$\frac{3}{4}$ cup
caster sugar	90g/3oz/$\frac{1}{3}$ cup
large eggs, beaten	3

TO MAKE A SWISS ROLL SPONGE

1 Preheat the oven to 220C/425F/Gas 7. Grease and line a 30 × 20cm/12 × 8in Swiss roll tin (pan) or rectangular tin with non-stick paper (see illustrations 1 and 2, left).

2 Sift the flour twice onto a piece of greaseproof (waxed) paper.

3 Put the sugar and eggs in a large greasefree bowl over a pan of gently simmering water and whisk until the mixture is thick and leaves a thin trail when the whisk is lifted.

4 Carefully fold in the flour with a metal spoon: use a figure-of-eight movement and stop folding as soon as the flour has been incorporated. Take care not to over-mix.

5 Quickly pour the mixture into the prepared tin and gently tap the sides to level. Do not level with a spoon.

6 Bake for 6-8 minutes until the sponge is pale golden brown and springs back when pressed lightly with a finger. Take care not to overcook otherwise the texture will be spoilt.

7 While the cake is cooking prepare a surface for rolling: lay a large piece of greaseproof paper over a damp cloth and lightly sprinkle the paper with caster sugar. Have ready another piece of greaseproof paper.

8 As soon as the cake is cooked, turn out onto the prepared paper and remove cake lining paper.

TO ROLL THE SPONGE TIGHTLY
For using with a filling

1 Trim the cake edges. Make a shallow cut 1cm/$\frac{1}{2}$in in from the edge of the cake along one side (see illustration 1, page 8). For rolling the sponge widthwise, cut the strip along a short side;

Rolling Swiss Roll Sponge Tightly

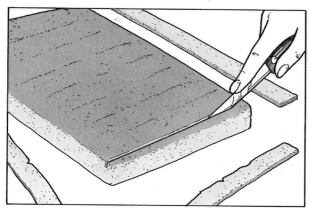

1 Trim the edges, then make a shallow cut 1cm/½in in from the edge to be rolled.

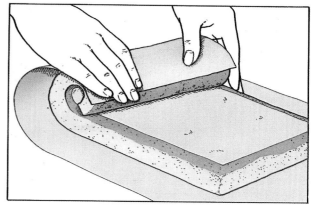

2 Roll up the sponge and top paper from cut side; pull the underpaper with one hand.

for rolling lengthwise, cut the strip down a long side.

2 To roll the sponge widthwise, place a piece of greaseproof (waxed) paper on top of the cake and roll up the cake (including the top paper) from the cut short side, pulling the underpaper with one hand and guiding the roll with the other hand (see illustration 2, above).

3 To roll the sponge lengthwise, roll up as described in step 2 above, but start from the cut long side.

4 Gently pull off the outer paper. Make sure join is underneath, cover loosely and leave to cool. Use the same day.

TO ROLL THE SPONGE LOOSELY
For wrapping around another cake

1 Lightly oil a milk or wine bottle, then wrap neatly with a layer of greaseproof (waxed) paper. Lightly oil the paper.

2 Trim the edges of the cake and place a piece of greaseproof paper on top of the cake. Lay the prepared bottle at one end and roll the cake (including the top paper) around the bottle, pulling the underpaper with one hand and guiding the roll with the other hand.

3 Gently pull off the outer paper, cover loosely and leave to cool. Use the same day.

FOOD COLOURING

Food colouring is available in paste, powder and liquid form. Use as follows:

Paste: for colouring sugarpaste, marzipan and buttercream; for painting onto sugarpaste.

Powder: for colouring marzipan, buttercream, white chocolate, fudge icing, Italian frosting and small quantities of sugarpaste; for brushwork and tinting rice paper.

Liquid: for colouring buttercream, Italian frosting, white fudge icing and tiny quantities of sugarpaste.

Colouring pens
These are similar in appearance to thin felt-tipped pens and are used for drawing on dry sugarpaste. They are available in various colours from specialist cake decorating shops. Use instead of a paint brush to mark features or write names on the cakes.

THE ICINGS

A variety of icings are used to fill and cover the dinosaur cakes, giving each cake an individual look and taste.

Buttercream is the best icing for sandwiching layers of cake together and for sticking pieces in position. It can be made in advance and flavoured as desired. To add interest to a cake, try mixing the flavours – for instance, use an orange-flavoured buttercream to sandwich a chocolate-flavoured sponge together. Chocolate fudge icing may be used instead of buttercream, but it cannot be made in advance.

For covering the simpler cakes buttercream, fudge icing and Italian frosting are suitable, but for a more professional finish sugarpaste is the best choice. It also has the advantage of keeping the cake underneath moist, and is useful for making decorative features. When sugarpaste dries out it can become quite brittle.

Ready-made sugarpaste is also known as plastic icing or fondant icing in Australia. It can be bought from most supermarkets in 500g/1lb packets or in larger quantities from specialist cake decorating shops.

A ready-to-roll icing is available under trade names but this is sweeter and softer in texture than sugarpaste and should be kneaded with a little extra icing sugar if used for covering cakes.

Marzipan

Use white marzipan, if possible; yellow marzipan is difficult to colour successfully. Colour and use marzipan as for quick sugarpaste.

Chocolate fudge icing

Ingredients	basic quantity
plain chocolate	125g/4oz
butter	60g/2oz
egg, beaten	1
icing (confectioner's) sugar, sifted	185g/6oz/1 cup

TO MAKE CHOCOLATE FUDGE ICING

1 Have the cake ready before starting the icing.
2 Break up the chocolate and place in a bowl with the butter.
3 Place the bowl over hot water until the chocolate has melted. Alternatively, melt the chocolate and butter in the microwave – refer to manufacturer's handbook for timings.
4 Beat in the egg, remove the bowl from the heat and stir in half the sugar.
5 Beat in the remaining sugar and continue to beat until the icing is creamy and cold.
6 Use the icing immediately for spreading inside the cake, or leave for a few minutes before using to cover the cake.

● An eggless version may be made by substituting 2 tablespoons milk for the egg and whisking hard with an electric beater until smooth.

White fudge icing

Ingredients	basic quantity
white chocolate	125g/4oz
butter	60g/2oz
icing (confectioner's) sugar, sifted	185g/6oz/1 cup
milk	about 3 tbsp

TO MAKE WHITE FUDGE ICING

1 Have the cake ready before starting to make the icing.
2 Break up the chocolate and place in a bowl.
3 Place the bowl over hot water until chocolate has melted. Alternatively, melt chocolate in microwave – refer to manufacturer's handbook.
4 Meanwhile, melt the butter in another bowl over hot water or in the microwave.
5 Add the sugar, melted butter and milk to the melted chocolate and immediately beat well until the icing is smooth and forms soft peaks. Add a little more milk if necessary. Add food colouring, if using.
6 Use the icing immediately.

Buttercream

Ingredients	250g/8oz quantity	500g/1lb quantity
icing (confectioner's) sugar	250g/8oz/ 1½ cups	500g/1lb/ 3 cups
*butter, softened	125g/4oz	250g/8oz
milk	2 tbsp	3 tbsp

Flavourings – add one of the following:

drinking chocolate powder	30g/1oz/ ¼ cup	60g/2oz/ ½ cup
*juice and grated rind of lemon	½ lemon	1 lemon
*juice and grated rind of orange	½ orange	1 orange

* Replace the milk with the juice, or omit if using a soft spreading fat instead of butter.

TO MAKE BUTTERCREAM

1 Sift the sugar and chocolate powder, if using, into a bowl.
2 In another bowl, blend the butter with the milk, or juice if using; gradually work in the sugar.
3 Beat the mixture for several minutes until light and fluffy. Add food colouring, if using. Alternatively, blend all the ingredients in a blender or food processor; if necessary add a little more liquid.

Italian frosting

Ingredients	1-egg quantity	2-egg quantity
eggs	1	2
icing (confectioner's) sugar, sifted	90g/3oz/ ½ cup	185g/6oz/ 1 cup

TO MAKE ITALIAN FROSTING

1 Have the cake ready before starting the icing.
2 Place the egg(s) and sugar in a bowl over a pan of hot water.
3 Whisk the mixture until thick, then add food colouring, if using, and continue to whisk until icing stands up in stiff peaks. Use immediately.

Quick sugarpaste

Ingredients	500g/1lb quantity
liquid glucose	6 tsp
glycerine	1 tsp
egg white	1 large
icing (confectioner's) sugar, sifted	500g/1lb/3 cups

TO MAKE QUICK SUGARPASTE

1 Measure the liquid glucose with a dry warm spoon and place in a large dry warm bowl with the glycerine and egg white. (Liquid glucose and glycerine can be bought from chemist shops.)
2 Beat the ingredients lightly, then stir in three-quarters of the sugar and mix well.
3 Knead in enough of the remaining sugar to make a firm smooth malleable paste.
4 Knead the paste well on a clean, dry surface that has been lightly dusted with icing sugar, then wrap in several layers of plastic wrap and leave for 4-8 hours before using. Do not refrigerate.
5 Always keep the sugarpaste well wrapped when not in use, as it tends to dry out quickly. If it does dry out, sprinkle with a little cooled boiled water, wrap in several layers of plastic wrap and leave for 4-8 hours to soften.

TO COLOUR SUGARPASTE
For pastel shades

1 Break off a small piece of sugarpaste and colour with a little food colouring paste or powder. Break off small pieces of the coloured sugarpaste and knead gradually into the main piece until the required shade is achieved.

For dark shades

1 Cut the sugarpaste into several slices and spread the cut surfaces with food colouring paste. Sandwich back together and knead on a surface sprinkled with icing sugar until evenly coloured. Wear thin plastic gloves while kneading to avoid staining hands.
2 Repeat this process until required depth of colour is achieved. (The colour will intensify after a few minutes.) Do not overknead.

3 To colour large quantities, work in 2–3 batches, then lightly knead together for an even shade.

For a mottled effect

1 This method uses less colouring and can be applied to any of the sugarpaste-covered cakes.
2 First cover the cake with white sugarpaste. Cover your finger with kitchen paper or fine linen and lightly smear paste colouring onto sugarpaste. Blot dry with kitchen paper. Alternatively, brush powder colouring onto sugarpaste with a clean pastry brush.

DECORATIONS

Small sweets are handy for creating decorative features, such as eyes, but avoid bright ones as the colour may bleed onto the icing.

Ice cream cones and wafers are excellent for horns, fans and tails and they are readily available from supermarkets.

CHOCOLATE

Choose good quality brown or white melting chocolate, which is available as buttons or in blocks. Dessert chocolate can be used in icings or simply grated for decorative purposes, but it is too brittle to be used for run-out designs.

White chocolate has slightly different properties to brown chocolate, but it can be tinted or flavoured as required.

To melt chocolate, place broken pieces in a bowl over a pan of hot water. Leave for 2–4 minutes until chocolate is soft. Alternatively, melt in the microwave – refer to the manufacturer's handbook.

To colour white chocolate, sprinkle a few grains of food colouring powder over the melted chocolate, then mix in. Colouring paste can be used for small quantities; stir well.

RICE PAPER

Rice paper is available in small sheets from supermarkets and specialist cake decorating shops, but larger, stronger sheets can often be purchased from bakeries. Keep dry and flat, and colour only with powder.

ASSEMBLING THE CAKES

Impressive novelty cakes are easy to create once you've mastered a few basic techniques.

TO MAKE TEMPLATES

1 To size up the pattern pieces, mark out 1cm/½in squares on graph paper and copy the pieces, square by square. When the pieces are drawn, trace them onto thin cardboard – cereal box cardboard is ideal. Alternatively, draw up a grid of 1cm/½in squares directly onto the cardboard, then copy the pieces onto the grid.
2 Label and number the pieces as shown *before* cutting them out.

TO SLICE A CAKE HORIZONTALLY

1 Place one hand lightly on top of the cake and, using a large serrated knife with the blade held flat, cut a little way through the thickness. Rotate the cake and continue to cut all the way round. Repeat, slicing through to the centre of the cake.
2 Carefully lift off the top layer and place on the table, top side uppermost.
3 Spread the base with icing and replace the top. The filling keeps the cake moist.

TEMPLATE FOR LEGS

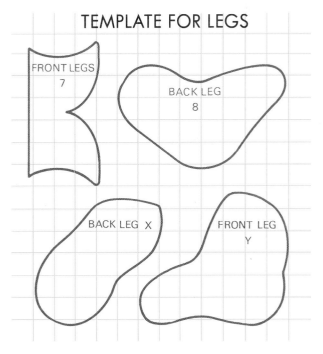

FRONT LEGS
7

BACK LEG
8

BACK LEG X

FRONT LEG
Y

TO SHAPE THE CAKE

1 Trim a thin layer off the top of the cakes to flatten if necessary.

2 Cut the cakes into pieces following instructions and illustrations given in individual recipes. To cut pieces using the templates, place the templates on the surface of the cake as shown in individual recipes, then cut round with a sharp pointed knife; hold the template firmly in place with one hand as you cut.

3 Stack the pieces of cake on the cakeboard to form the body, then stick together with icing. Cover the cake with foil and leave to set for at least 30 minutes.

Remember to save a little buttercream for use later in the recipe.

4 Cut the cake to shape by shaving off thin slices, using a small serrated knife and cutting downwards towards the board. Any mistakes can be built back onto the cake with icing.

5 Round off sharp edges along the back.

6 Cut the base of the dinosaur inwards, away from the board, so that the icing can be tucked underneath.

TO MAKE THE TAIL

1 Most of the tails are made from leftover pieces of cake. If the pieces do not fit exactly, simply cut to fit and re-position; fill joins and gaps with buttercream.

2 Assemble the tail in a straight line and shave off the sharp edges along the length using a small serated knife.

3 If covering with sugarpaste, trim the tail well at the base so that the sugarpaste can be tucked underneath to help lift the tail off the board slightly.

4 To curve the tail, cut out small triangles of cake along one side of the trimmed tail and then close up the pieces of cake to form the curve. Stick with icing.

TO PREPARE THE CAKE FOR DECORATING

1 Brush away the loose crumbs.

2 Slacken a little buttercream with milk or juice and spread thinly over all the cut surfaces using a small round-bladed or flexible knife.

3 Spread a little icing over the remaining cake and wipe the board clean.

TO COVER WITH SUGARPASTE

1 Lightly sprinkle sifted icing (confectioner's) sugar onto a clean dry surface. Using a grease-free rolling pin, roll out the sugarpaste as for thick pastry. (Special boards and rolling pins are available from specialist cake decorating shops.) Any air bubbles can be removed by pricking with a pin.

2 Support the rolled-out sugarpaste with your hands, or with the rolling pin, and carefully transfer to the cake.

3 Using clean dry hands dusted with icing sugar or cornflour (cornstarch), smooth the sugarpaste over the cake. Polish the sugarpaste with the flat of the hand in a smooth circular movement.

4 Trim the sugarpaste at the base of the cake. Gather up and wrap all the trimmings and do not discard until the cake is completed as these are often used for moulding horns or claws at the end of the recipe.

5 Smooth over any marks, splits or joins, by stroking the sugarpaste with a round-bladed knife, and then your finger.

6 Using the handle of a spoon, push the cut edge under the cake to neaten.

7 To give texture to the sugarpaste, mark while still soft with forks, spoon handles, straws or graters.

8 Freshly-rolled sugarpaste will stick to itself, but when adding to a dry surface, use cooled boiled water or pure alcohol to moisten.

TO COVER WITH SOFT ICING

1 Using a round-bladed knife, spread buttercream or fudge icing onto the surface of the cake. To help Italian frosting stick to the cake, brush the cake first with a little warmed and sieved jam, rather than a thin layer of buttercream.

2 Spread the icing in clean strokes. To give a smooth finish to buttercream, run a warm round-bladed knife over the surface.

3 Any left-over buttercream can be spread on the cakeboard to give a decorative finish to the board.

STORING THE CAKE

The basic cakes can be made in advance and stored in the freezer until ready to assemble – wrap well, label and freeze for up to two months.

To thaw the cakes, unwrap and leave at room temperature for 1-2 hours.

Upright cakes may be completed in advance, depending on the type of icing used –
Italian frosting and fudge icing: 1-2 days in advance
Buttercream: 2-3 days in advance

Sugarpaste: 4-5 days in advance

Decorated flat cakes may be frozen. First check that you have room for the cakeboard in the freezer. Open-freeze the cake, then cover loosely in foil until required. To thaw, remove from the freezer twenty-four hours before serving and leave, uncovered, at room temperature. The sugarpaste will appear wet on thawing, but will dry off within a few hours in a warm dry room.

Making Horns

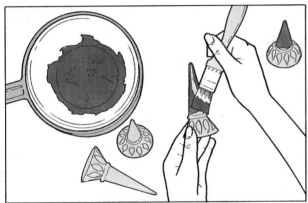

1 For chocolate horns, brush melted chocolate thickly over pointed ends of cones. Dry, then cover with another layer.

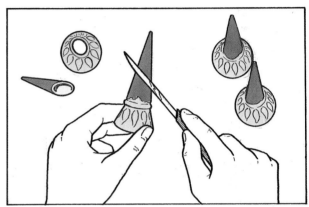

2 When the chocolate is dry but not hard, mark a cutting line all round with a pointed knife. Most are cut on a slant.

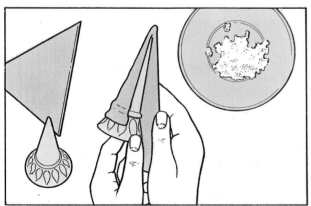

3 For sugarpaste horns, cut a triangle of sugarpaste to size, moisten with a damp brush and mould round cone; smooth join.

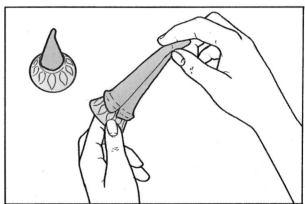

4 Leave the end rounded or pull and mould into a hooked shape. Mark a cutting line all round with a pointed knife.

· S T Y R A C O S A U R U S ·

sty-rak-oh-*saw*-rus

The Styracosaurus had a large horn on its snout and a formidable-looking spiky frill which covered much of its neck. This impressive array would have frightened off most predators or rivals of the same species.

SERVES 20-25
LENGTH: 45cm/18in

Allow plenty of time to assemble this cake. Make the horns the day before, if possible.

CAKES

2 rectangular cakes (see page 5)
1 fairy bun, made with 1 tablespoon sponge mixture (see page 5)

ICING

750g/1½lb buttercream (see page 10)
2.5kg/5lb quick sugarpaste (see page 10)

FOOD COLOURING

purple, pink, yellow, orange and *green* paste food colouring

DECORATION

7 ice cream wafer cones

TO SHAPE THE BODY

1 Cut the cakes into four pieces (see illustration 1, page 16).
2 Stack pieces A, B and C on the board, placing piece A on the bottom and graduating them in 2.5cm/1in steps at the front. Stick together with buttercream and leave to set.
3 Cut off the corners of the cake with a serrated knife and trim to make the shape of the body (see illustrations 2 and 3). Use the trimmings to build up the curved back and stick in place with buttercream (see illustration 3). Cut the base of the cake inwards away from the board.

TO SHAPE THE TAIL

1 Cut the remaining piece of cake into the tail pieces (see illustration 3).
2 Slice horizontally through pieces X, Y and Z. Assemble the tail pieces at the back (see illustration 4). Stick in position with buttercream.
3 Trim and shape the tail along the length and cut the base of the tail inwards, away from the board.
4 Curve the tail (see illustration 4).

TO COLOUR THE ICING

1 Colour 185g/6oz sugarpaste *purple*.
2 Colour 1.75kg/3½lb sugarpaste deep *pink*.
3 Colour 125g/4oz sugarpaste *yellow*.
4 Colour 30g/1oz sugarpaste *orange*.
5 Colour 30g/1oz sugarpaste *green*.
6 Leave the remaining sugarpaste *white*.

TO MAKE THE HORNS

1 Cover the pointed tips of the ice cream cones with *purple* sugarpaste (see page 13) and leave until completely dry.
2 Cut diagonally across the wide ends of the

Shaping And Assembling Styracosaurus

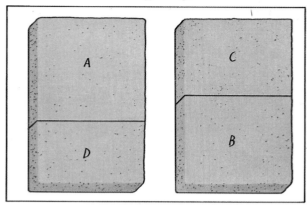

1 Using a sharp knife, cut the cakes into pieces A, B, C and D.

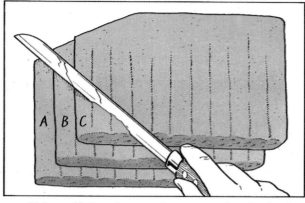

2 Trim off the sharp edges to make the body; round off the front and slope the back.

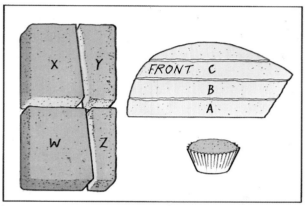

3 Build up the curved back with trimmings. Cut D into tail pieces W, X, Y and Z.

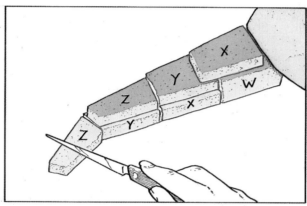

4 Assemble the tail at back of body and curve by cutting out triangular sections.

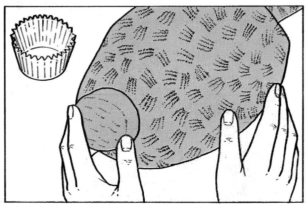

5 Stick the bun onto the front of the dinosaur to make the face.

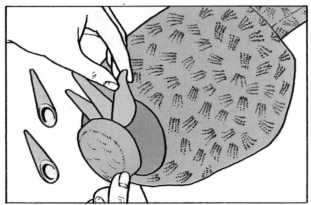

6 Gently push the horns into the sugarpaste roll, positioning the largest at the top.

cones so that the shortest sides measure as follows:

two cones × 6cm/2½in;

two cones × 5cm/2in;

two cones × 3.5cm/1½in.

3 Cut straight across the base of the remaining cone to make a 5cm/2in long central horn.

TO COVER THE CAKE

1 Spread a thin layer of buttercream over the cake and fairy bun.

2 Roll out 60g/2oz *white* sugarpaste thickly and wrap it all round the bun, smoothing over the join.

3 Roll out 125g/4oz *white* sugarpaste thickly and smooth it over the top of the cake to give a smooth

TEMPLATE FOR STYRACOSAURUS

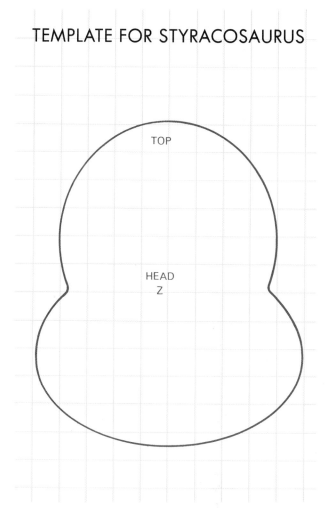

rounded back to the dinosaur.

4 Reserve 500g/1lb *pink* sugarpaste and roll out remainder to cover the body and tail. Smooth the sugarpaste over the cake and tail and trim the base, pushing the edge underneath to neaten. Alternatively, cover the body and tail separately and smooth the join with a knife and then the fingers, to neaten.

5 Mark all over the body and tail with a modelling tool or fork.

6 Roll out 440g/14oz *pink* sugarpaste thickly. Using templates X and Y (see page 11), cut out two front legs and two back legs. Mould onto the body and mark with the modelling tool.

7 Stick the bun onto the front of the dinosaur to form the face and leave to set for 30 minutes (see illustration 5).

TO MAKE THE FACE

1 Reserve a pea-sized piece of *pink* sugarpaste and gather up the remaining trimmings. Make up to 90g/3oz with *white* sugarpaste. Mould the sugarpaste into a sausage about 13cm/5in long and press around the top half of the bun, moistening with a little water if necessary.

2 Gently push the trimmed horns into the soft sugarpaste sausage, placing the smallest ones at the base and the largest ones at the top (see illustration 6).

3 Roll out the *yellow* sugarpaste thickly. Using template Z, cut out the face and place it in position so that it rests just above the base of the horns and covers the bun. Mould the sugarpaste round underneath the bun.

4 Mark the nostrils with the modelling tool and push the remaining horn into position through the soft sugarpaste.

5 Shape the reserved *pink* sugarpaste into two thin strands and place in position radiating out from the nose.

6 Mould the *orange* sugarpaste into a bill and press into position.

7 Mould the *green* sugarpaste into claws and stick onto the feet. Use black colouring to paint on the eyes.

•PENTACERATOPS•

pen-ta-ser-a-tops

Like the Chasmosaurus (page 55), the Pentaceratops had a huge neck frill fringed with small spines. It had three horns on its face and protruding cheek bones which gave the appearance of horns.

SERVES 20-25
LENGTH: 48cm/19in

Do not make the white fudge icing until you are ready to use it.

CAKES

1 pudding bowl cake, made in a 1.25 litre/ 40fl oz/5 cup bowl (see page 6)
1 pudding bowl cake, made in a 1.57 litre/ 50fl oz/6 cup bowl (see page 6)

ICING

500g/1lb buttercream (see page 10)
1 quantity *white* fudge icing (see page 9)
500g/1lb chocolate-flavoured sugarpaste or *white* quick sugarpaste, coloured *brown*

FOOD COLOURING

brown and *black* paste, liquid or powder food colouring

DECORATION

3 ice cream wafer cones
grated chocolate or chocolate chips
185g/6oz white chocolate (see page 11)

TO SHAPE THE CAKE

1 Trim the tops off the cakes, if neccessary. Slice through the small cake horizontally three times and through the large cake four times (see illustration 1, page 20). Sandwich the slices back together again with buttercream.
2 Place the large cake, wide end down, on the board to make the body.
3 Invert the small cake, so that it is wide end up, and cut into three pieces (see illustration 2). Remove the top layer from the head, piece A.
4 Cut this layer in half and stick the smaller piece on top of the head; trim the sharp edges (see illustration 3). Slice away the top crust of the larger piece and reserve the piece for the fan.
5 Divide pieces B and C into four and use for the tail (see illustrations 4 and 5).
6 Trim a small slice off the front of the body cake and stick on top of cake (see illustration 5).

TO COVER THE BODY

1 Make up the white fudge icing and tint with a few drops of *brown* colouring. Spread about two-thirds icing over the body and tail of the dinosaur, swirling with a knife.
2 Sprinkle grated chocolate or chocolate chips over the icing and press lightly to stick.

TO COVER THE HEAD AND FAN

1 Spread the head and fan with buttercream.
2 Roll out 250g/8oz chocolate-flavoured sugarpaste into a 25cm/10in circle and smooth over the head. Trim where necessary but leave a little all

Shaping And Assembling Pentaceratops

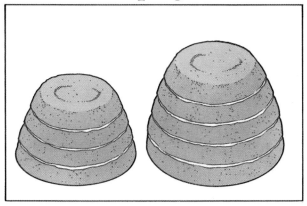

1 *Slice through small cake 3 times and large cake 4 times. Stick back together.*

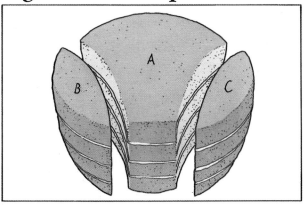

2 *Stand the small cake wide end uppermost and cut into shape. Remove a layer from A.*

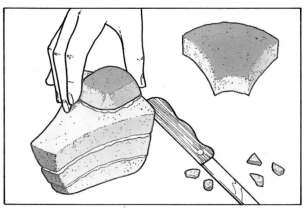

3 *Cut the single layer in half and stick the smaller piece on top of the head (A).*

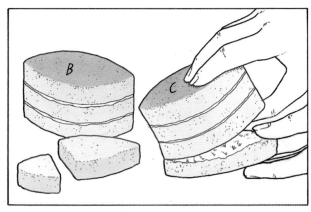

4 *Split up B and C to make four tail pieces; trim the small pieces to fit the tail.*

5 *Stick the tail together. Slice a small piece from front of body cake and stick on top.*

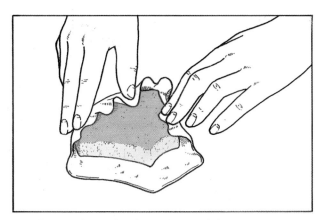

6 *Cover the cake fan piece with sugarpaste, taking the excess onto the other side.*

round to tuck and stick under. Place head on body.

3 Gather up the trimmings and make up to 30g/1oz from the reserved sugarpaste. Mould two short fat horns and stick onto the cheek bones. Smooth the joins.

4 Make a template of the fan. Roll out the remaining sugarpaste thinly and cut out two fan shapes. Lightly roll one piece to enlarge slightly, then cover in plastic wrap and reserve.

5 Cut a third fan shape, allowing a 2.5cm/1in margin all round. Smooth it over the top and sides of the fan-shaped piece of cake. Tuck the excess underneath, smoothing out the creases and sticking where necessary (see illustration 6).

6 Lay the smaller sugarpaste fan shape on the underside and press firmly to neaten. This will be the back of the fan. Position the fan behind the head, resting on the body, and gently ease down the sugarpaste on either side to fill any gaps between head, body and fan. Lift off the fan and head and leave to set.

TO MAKE THE HORNS AND FAN

1 On plain or graph paper, mark out a grid to give at least ten 2.5cm/1in squares. Extend the lines at each side to use as a cutting guide. Stick the paper onto a flat surface and stick a smooth piece of waxed or non-stick paper on top.

2 Melt the *white* chocolate in a bowl over hot water or in the microwave. Do not overheat.

3 Pour one-third of the chocolate into another bowl and colour *brown*. Pour this chocolate onto the prepared paper and tap the paper to spread the chocolate evenly, leaving the extended lines visible. Leave to set.

4 Brush some of the *white* chocolate over the ice cream cones to make the horns (see page 13). Mark a diagonal line across the wide ends of two cones so that the shortest sides measure 6cm/2½in. Mark straight across the base of the remaining cone to make a 5cm/2in central horn. Leave to set.

5 Reheat the remaining *white* chocolate if necessary, and brush thickly over the front and down each side of the fan. Allow this layer to set slightly before applying the next. Repeat until about 1 teaspoon chocolate remains.

6 Roll the sugarpaste trimmings into three very thin strips and press lightly onto the front of the fan. Leave the fan to set.

TO FINISH THE CAKE

1 With a long knife, cut the chocolate spread on the paper using the guide-lines to make squares.

2 Spread a little melted chocolate diagonally across each square and press onto the back of the fan so that the points are visible from the front of the cake (see illustration below).

3 (This step may be omitted if wished). To neaten, spread the reserved sugarpaste fan shape with buttercream or jam. Lay the chocolate-coated fan, back side down, on top of the sugarpaste. Lift up the fan, smooth the back where necessary and place the head and fan on the cake.

4 Cut through the ice cream cones where marked, and press the horns firmly in place through the soft sugarpaste on the head. If the sugarpaste has set too hard, cut a circle out with the point of a small sharp knife.

5 Use any remaining sugarpaste trimmings to make the claws.

6 Paint or mark on the nostrils and eyes.

Finishing The Fan

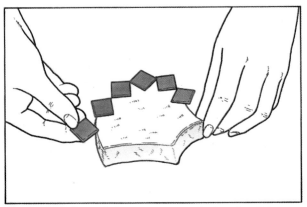

Press the chocolate squares onto back of fan so that points are visible from front.

·YANGCHUANOSAURUS·

yang-*chwan*-oh-*saw*-rus

*The Yangchuanosaurus had a large head with a
powerful jaw. Inside the mouth were large sharp fangs
that curved backwards – each fang was serrated rather
like a kitchen knife. The thick heavy tail helped to
support the dinosaur's body weight.*

SERVES 15-20
LENGTH: 45cm/18in

This cake is assembled in the same way as a jigsaw
– the individual pieces of cake are slotted together
to make up the shape of the dinosaur. To ensure
that the pieces fit well, cover the cake thinly and
evenly.

CAKES

1 rectangular cake (see page 5)
1 round 23cm/9in cake (see page 5)

ICING

500g/1lb buttercream (see page 10)
1kg/2lb quick sugarpaste (see page 10)

FOOD COLOURING

green paste food colouring

TO SHAPE THE CAKE

1 Slice horizontally through the cakes and sandwich back together again with a little
buttercream.
2 Make templates A to J (see page 24) and place
them on the cakes as shown. Using a sharp knife,
cut round the templates.
3 Stick pieces A and B together with a little
buttercream to make the back. Stick pieces E and
F together to make the leg.

TO COLOUR THE ICING

1 Colour 375g/12oz sugarpaste very dark *green*.
2 Leave the remainder *white*; this is coloured at a
later stage.

TO COVER THE CAKE

1 Spread a thin layer of buttercream over each
piece of cake and leave the pieces spread out.
2 Roll out 125g/4oz *green* sugarpaste thickly.
Using templates G and H, cut out the back leg
shapes, leaving a 2.5cm/1in margin all round.

Assembling The Cake

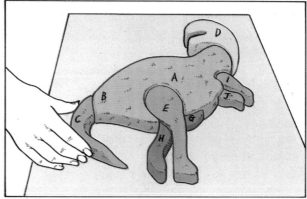

*Taking care not to dent the icing, move the
cake pieces into position on the board.*

TEMPLATE FOR YANGCHUANOSAURUS

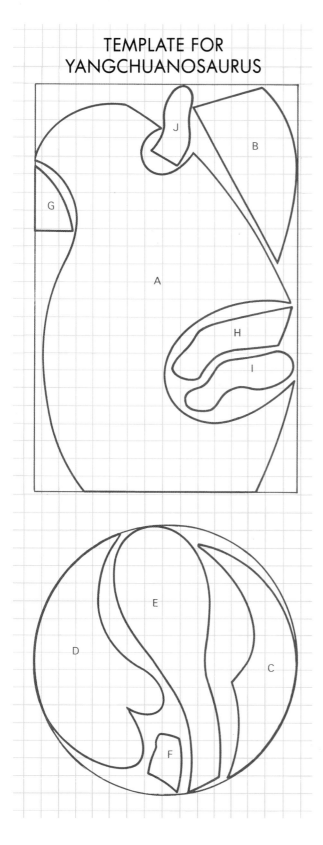

Smooth the sugarpaste over the top and sides of the matching cake pieces. Push the edges under to neaten. Reserve a large pea-sized piece of *green* sugarpaste for the mouth.*

3 Knead the remaining *green* sugarpaste into 250g/8oz *white* sugarpaste to make a paler *green* shade and roll out 315g/10oz thinly. Cut out the back leg (E and F) in one piece, the tail (C) and front legs (I and J), leaving a 2.5cm/1in margin all round. Smooth the sugarpaste over the top and sides of the matching cake pieces and push the edges under to neaten.

4 Knead the remaining *green* sugarpaste into another 250g/8oz *white* sugarpaste to make a paler shade. Cut out the body (A and B) in one piece, leaving a 2.5cm/1in margin all round. Place the body cake pieces in position on the board and cover with the sugarpaste. Push the edges under to neaten.

5 Knead the remaining pieces of *green* sugarpaste into the remaining *white* sugarpaste. Cut out the head (D), leaving a 2.5cm/1in margin all round. Smooth the sugarpaste over the top and sides of the matching cake piece and push the edges under to neaten.

6 Check that the pieces fit together (see illustration, page 22): to achieve a snug fit you may need to brush your finger down the side of certain pieces to thin out the sugarpaste.

7 Leave to set for about 15 minutes before reassembling.

TO FINISH THE CAKE

1 Carefully push the pieces of cake into position on the board (see illustration, page 22).
2 Roll the reserved piece of dark *green* sugarpaste into a narrow strip about 6cm/2½in long, tapering down to a point at one end. Snip along each side to represent teeth and stick in position, bending the strip up from the board and across the head to represent the mouth.
3 Paint on the eye.

*Alternatively, paint on the mouth.

·IGUANODON·

ig-*wa*-no-*don*

This plant-eater had strong hind legs and was able to walk upright as well as on all fours. The Iguanodon's defensive weapons were its long front claws which were formed into pointed spikes.

SERVES 20-25
LENGTH: 55cm/22in

CAKES

2 rectangular cakes (see page 5)

ICING

500g/1lb buttercream (see page 10)
2kg/4lb quick sugarpaste (see page 10)

FOOD COLOURING

yellow, orange and *green* paste or powder food colouring
black paste food colouring

TO SHAPE THE CAKE

1 Cut the cakes (see illustration 1, page 27), then stick the body piece A, B, and C together with buttercream, making sure that the middle piece extends 3.5cm/1½in out at the back.
2 Place the body on the board and stick the tail pieces together (see illustration 2).
3 Trim off the sharp edges to shape the body and tail. Cut the base of the cake inwards and away from the board.
4 Cut a 3.5cm/1½in piece off F and stick on top of piece D to make the raised forehead of the dinosaur (see illustration 3). Split through the remaining piece F at an angle and stick onto piece E, positioning the highest side 2.5cm/1in back from one end, to make the lower jaw (see illustration 3).

TO COLOUR THE ICING

1 Colour 60g/2oz sugarpaste *yellow*.
2 Colour 185g/6oz sugarpaste *black* and leave the remainder *white*.

TO COVER THE CAKE

1 Cover the body and tail with buttercream.
2 Roll out 875g/1¾lb *white* sugarpaste to a strip about 50cm/20in long and 30cm/12in wide at one end, tapering down to 5cm/2in at the other end.
3 Press a grater or wire sieve firmly over the sugarpaste to mark. Smooth the sugarpaste over the body and tail, easing it between the legs at the front. Trim edges and push under to neaten.
4 Roll out 125g/4oz *white* sugarpaste thickly and cut out two strips 10 × 7.5cm/4 × 3in. Mark with the grater or sieve, then wrap lengthwise around the front legs leaving about 2.5cm/1in to lie flat on the board. Cut four long slits on each foot.
5 Roll out 125g/4oz *white* sugarpaste. Mould two back legs, mark with the grater or sieve and stick into position on the cake. Leave to set.

TO MAKE THE HEAD

1 Cover cake head pieces with buttercream.
2 Roll out the *black* sugarpaste thickly and use to cover the lower jaw, pushing the excess under.
3 Roll out 185g/6oz *white* sugarpaste into a strip 38 × 3.5cm/15 × 1½in. Moisten the sides of the lower jaw and press the strip in place so that the

Shaping And Assembling Iguanodon

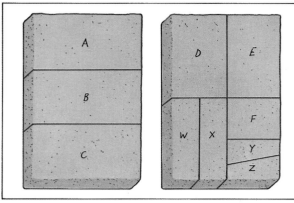

1 Using a large serrated knife, cut the two cakes into the body and tail pieces.

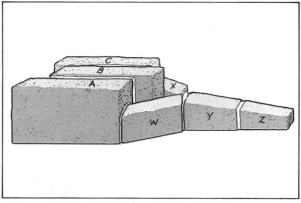

2 Stick the body pieces together, making B extend out at back. Assemble the tail.

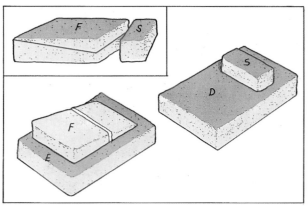

3 Cut a 3.5cm/1½in piece (S) from F; stick onto D. Split remaining F; stick onto E.

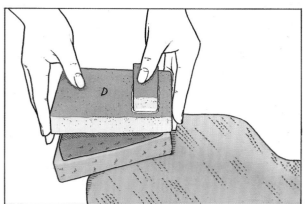

4 Place covered lower jaw (E) over front legs and position forehead piece (D) on top.

top edge forms the lip. Push excess under jaw.

4 Place the lower jaw onto the body positioning it well over the front legs. Place the forehead piece on top, slightly towards the back (see illustration 4). Place two small balls of sugarpaste near the front for nostrils.

5 Roll out 440g/14oz *white* sugarpaste into a strip 30cm/12in long and 20cm/8in wide at the front and 25cm/10in wide at the back. Mark with the grater or sieve.

6 Lay the strip over the head with the narrowest edge at the front. Fold the sugarpaste under the front of the mouth and tuck securely under to

make a lip. Mould carefully around the nostrils and brow, then down the back of the neck onto the body. Tuck under at side of mouth. Smooth over the join at the neck.

TO FINISH THE CAKE

1 Mould the *yellow* sugarpaste into claws. Use any remaining sugarpaste for teeth.

2 Brush *green* colouring lightly over the sugarpaste. Brush a strip of *orange* down the front between the legs and along the back.

3 Paint on the eyes and nostrils.

·ELASMOSAURUS·

ell-*as*-moh-*saw*-rus

The Elasmosaurus had flippers instead of legs and was able to glide along the sea in a graceful motion. Its long neck meant that it could easily catch fast-moving fish or even flying reptiles which skimmed the surface.

SERVES 20-25
LENGTH: 80cm/28in

This cake can be served on a shelf or plank of wood covered in blue icing to represent the sea. Mix 250g/8oz/1¼ cups icing (confectioner's) sugar with a little water until stiff for 'sea'.

CAKES

2 round 20cm/8in cakes (see page 5)
1 round 23cm/9in cake (see page 5)

ICING

375g/12oz buttercream (see page 10)
Italian frosting, made with 3 eggs (see page 10)

FOOD COLOURING

blue powder food colouring
yellow and *green* paste, liquid or powder food colouring

DECORATION

rice paper (see page 11)
edible silver balls
2 green jelly sweets

TO SHAPE THE CAKE

1 Slice horizontally through the cakes then sandwich back together with buttercream (optional). Sandwich the three cakes together with butter-cream, placing the largest in the middle.
2 Cut the cake in half and stand one half towards the end of the board. Trim both ends of the cake (see illustration 1, page 30).
3 Cut the second half of the cake into pieces X, Y and Z (see illustration 2). Stick piece X at the front of the main cake and piece Y at the back of the cake (see illustration 2).
4 Remove one layer of cake from piece Z, cut in half and sandwich the two pieces together for the head; trim into shape (see illustration 3).
5 Place the remaining piece of cake on the board 7.5cm/3in away from the body and trim either end to make the neck. Place the head 7.5cm/3in in front of the neck (see illustration 3).

TO MAKE THE FLIPPERS AND TAIL

1 Using a dry, clean pastry brush, evenly brush *blue* colouring over the rice paper. Repeat on reverse side of paper.
2 Using the templates (see page 30), cut out four flippers and two tail pieces.

TO COVER THE CAKE

1 Make up one quantity of Italian frosting, using two eggs. When stiff, remove 1 tablespoon and colour *green*. Colour remainder streaky *yellow*.
2 Spread the *yellow* frosting over top three-quarters of body and neck, and front half of head.
3 Make up another quantity of frosting, using one

Shaping Elasmosaurus

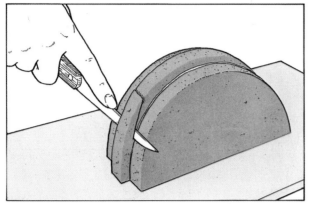

1 Place one half of assembled cake at end of board; level off sides of middle layer.

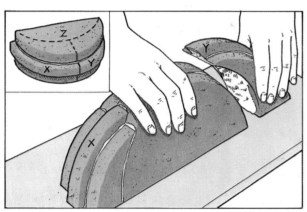

2 Cut the remaining cake half into X, Y and Z. Stick X and Y in place.

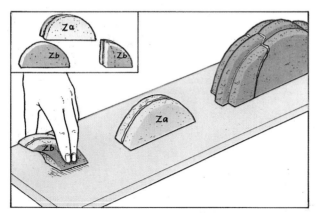

3 Cut one layer of Z in half, stick together and trim for the head. Place on board.

TEMPLATE FOR ELASMOSAURUS

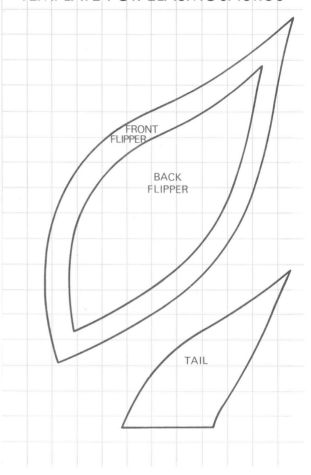

FRONT FLIPPER

BACK FLIPPER

TAIL

egg, and stir in a little *blue* colouring to tint.

4 Spread the *blue* frosting onto the sides of the cake, spreading down to the board.

5 Swirl a little *blue* and *green* frosting at random over the top of the cakes.

TO FINISH THE CAKE

1 Push the flippers into the side of the cake.

2 Scrape out the frosting bowl and use to stick the two paper tail pieces together. Place a small heap of buttercream on the board a little way from the back and push tail into position. Support for a few minutes with a crumpled kitchen towel.

3 Press silver balls into the cakes and use the green jelly sweets for eyes.

◆ CERATOSAURUS ◆

ser-a-toe-saw-rus

*The small narrow bony plates that ran down the back
and tail of the Ceratosaurus may have helped the
dinosaur in controlling its body temperature. The
massive jaw was filled with ferocious-looking teeth.*

SERVES 10-15
LENGTH: 40cm/16in

CAKES

1 rectangular cake (see page 5)

ICING

500g/1lb buttercream (see page 10)
125g/4oz quick sugarpaste (see page 10)

FOOD COLOURING

green paste or liquid food colouring
black paste or colouring pen (see page 8)

DECORATION

375g/12oz orange and lemon
jelly slices

TO SHAPE THE CAKE

1 Slice horizontally through the cake and sand-wich back together again with buttercream.
2 Make templates A, B, C, D, E and F (see page 33). Place on the cake as shown and cut round.
3 Arrange the pieces on the board and stick together (see illustration 1, page 33).

TO COLOUR THE ICING

1 Colour the sugarpaste a pale shade of *green*.
2 Colour the buttercream a pale shade of *green*.

TO COVER THE CAKE

1 Spread a thin layer of buttercream over cake.
2 Mould 30g/1oz *green* sugarpaste into a 15cm/6in sausage shape. Flatten each end for the hands, snip out three small V-shaped pieces and separate the fingers. Cut the sausage shape near the centre, making one piece slightly longer than the other.
3 Roll out the remaining *green* sugarpaste thinly. Cut out one piece 13 × 10cm/5 × 4in and smooth over the head onto the board. Trim to neaten.
5 Cut out two more pieces, each 10 × 5cm/4 × 2in. Smooth over the feet and trim.

TO FINISH THE CAKE

1 Spread the remaining buttercream thickly over the parts not covered with sugarpaste.
2 Place the two arms in position – the shorter one on the board and the longer one hanging down from the cake.
3 Cut some of the orange jelly sweets into tri-angular shapes (see illustration 2) and place along the back and tail, pressing the rounded edge of each shape into the buttercream. Press one shape onto the nose.
4 Arrange the remaining jelly slices over the body of the dinosaur in alternating rows of orange and lemon. Cut the slices in half for lower legs and tail.
5 Use the *black* colouring or pen to mark on the mouth and eye. Use remaining scraps of jelly for the claws.

Assembling And Finishing Ceratosaurus

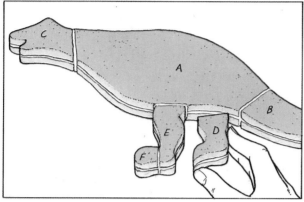

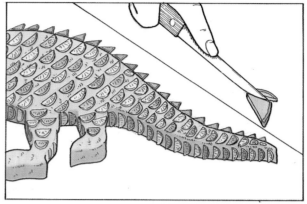

1 Arrange the cake pieces on the board to make the dinosaur shape.

2 Cut some jelly slices into pointed shapes and press into the top edge.

TEMPLATE FOR CERATOSAURUS

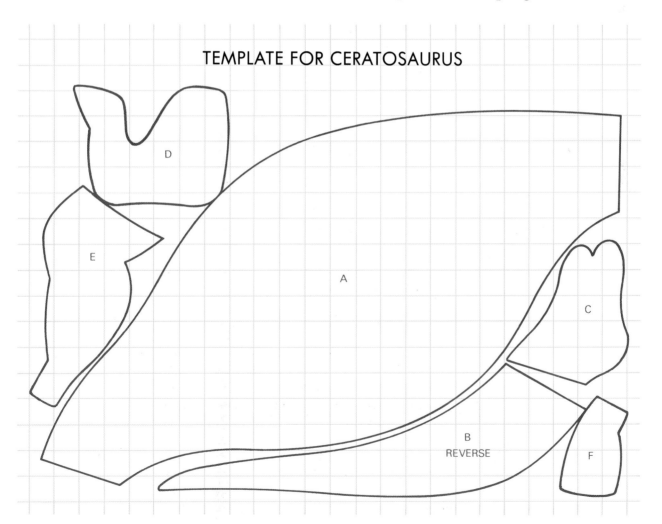

· EUOPLOCEPHALUS ·

yoo-*op*-low-*kef*-al-us

The impressive bony armoury covering the back and tail of this enormous plant-eater kept prowling meat-eaters at bay. The heavy club on the end of its tail was another excellent defence system.

SERVES 25-30
LENGTH: 55cm/22in

CAKES

2 round 20cm/8in cakes (see page 5)
1 round 23cm/9in cake (see page 5)

ICING

750g/1½lb buttercream (see page 10)
2kg/4lb quick sugarpaste (see page 10)

FOOD COLOURING

black and *green* paste food colouring

DECORATION

125g/4oz small iced biscuits or small jelly sweets

TO SHAPE THE BODY

1 Slice horizontally through the cakes and sandwich the two 20cm/8in cakes back together again with buttercream.
2 Stick one 23cm/9in layer between the two smaller cakes (see illustration 1, page 36).
3 Measuring from the edge of the top cake, cut off a 7.5cm/3in piece and cut into pieces (see illustration 2, page 36).
4 Position the main piece of cake on the board and trim one end. Attach piece X onto the trimmed end for the front (see illustration 3).

5 Cut the reserved layer (see illustration 4) and stick pieces 1 and 3 on either side of the body (see illustration 5). Cut piece 2 into three.

TO SHAPE THE TAIL

1 Split tail pieces Y and Z into three (see illustration 6), then assemble tail, pushing the small pointed pieces between the other pieces and curving the tail either forwards or backwards (see illustration 6); fill in any gaps with buttercream.
2 Cover the assembled cake with foil and leave to set.

TO COLOUR THE ICING

1 Colour 625g/1¼lb sugarpaste *black*.
2 Colour 30g/1oz sugarpaste *green* and leave the remainder *white*.

TO COVER THE CAKE

1 Trim off the sharp corners of the cake and cut the base of the dinosaur inwards away from the board.
2 Cover the cake with a thin layer of buttercream.
3 Roll out 1.25kg/2½lb *white* sugarpaste to a piece about 50cm/20in long and 30cm/12in wide at one end, tapering down to about 10cm/4in at the other end.
4 Smooth the sugarpaste over body and tail. Trim and push the edge under the cake to neaten.

Shaping And Assembling Euoplocephalus

1 *Sandwich one layer of the 23cm/9in cake between the two smaller cakes.*

2 *Measuring from the edge, cut off a 7.5cm/ 3in section and cut into X, Y and Z.*

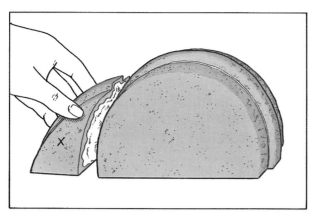

3 *Stand the main piece on the board, trim one end and attach X to make the front.*

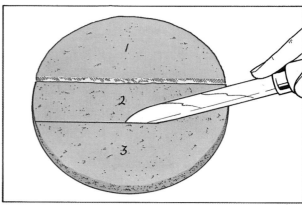

4 *Cut the remaining 23cm/9in layer of cake into three pieces.*

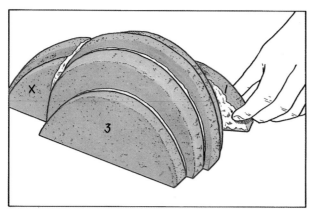

5 *Stick pieces 1 and 3 onto either side of the main body piece, pressing firmly in place.*

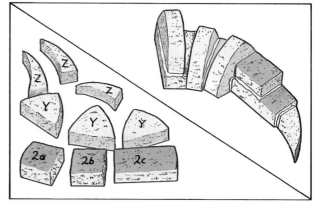

6 *Cut the remaining strip into three pieces, split up Y and Z and assemble the tail.*

TEMPLATE FOR EUOPLOCEPHALUS

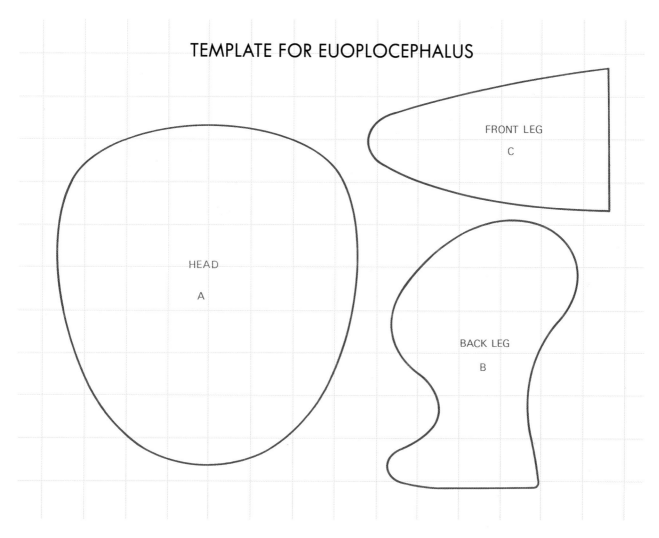

FRONT LEG

C

HEAD

A

BACK LEG

B

5 Roll out 500g/1lb *black* sugarpaste and cut into 30 × 3.5cm/12 × 1½in strips.

6 Lay the strips over the body and tail of the dinosaur, leaving a 3.5cm/1½in space between each one and starting 13cm/5in in from the front end of dinosaur.

7 Trim as necessary and re-roll the trimmings to cover the front end, starting 3.5cm/1½in away from the first black strip.

TO FINISH THE CAKE

1 Roll out remaining *white* sugarpaste thickly and, using template A, cut out the head. Stick in position.

2 Roll out the remaining *black* sugarpaste. Using templates B and C, cut out two front legs and two back legs. Stick them in position with about 2.5cm/1in lying flat on the board to represent the feet.

3 Gather together remaining *white* sugarpaste trimmings and use to roll into a ball for the end of the tail. Stick either onto the tail or onto the cakeboard.

4 Use the *green* sugarpaste to mould spikes and claws for the tail and feet. Cut 4 small diamonds for the top of the head.

5 Stick the biscuits or sweets onto the dinosaur with small spots of buttercream; position them in neat rows.

6 Use *black* colouring and a fine paint brush to paint on the face features.

•BRONTOSAURUS•

bron-toe-*saw*-rus

The giant Brontosaurus, otherwise known as Apatosaurus, was a plant-eater and had a small head perched on top of a long, powerful neck. Its long tail had a whip-like end used for fending off attackers.

SERVES 25-30
LENGTH: 60cm/24in

CAKES

2 rectangular cakes (see page 5)

ICING

750g/1½lb buttercream (see page 10)
250g/8oz quick sugarpaste (see page 10)

FOOD COLOURING

yellow, *orange* and *black* paste or liquid food colouring

DECORATION

yellow sugar mimosa balls

TO SHAPE THE CAKE

1 Cut the cakes (see illustration 1, page 40), then stack the pieces on the board, graduating them in 2.5cm/1in steps at the front of the dinosaur (see illustration 2).
2 Sandwich the pieces together with buttercream. Cover the cake with foil and leave to set for at least one hour.
3 Cut off the sharp edges of the cake to make the shape of the body.
4 Using a small pointed knife and template Z (see page 40), cut a hole through the cake to represent the curve of the neck (see illustration 2).

TO COLOUR THE ICING

1 Colour half the sugarpaste *yellow* and reserve a tiny ball for the toe nails.
2 Colour the remaining sugarpaste *pale orange*.
3 Colour the buttercream *pale orange*. Remove a quarter and colour *dark orange*.

TO COVER THE CAKE

1 Spread a thin layer of *pale orange* buttercream all over the cake and through the hole.
2 Spread the *dark orange* buttercream thickly along the back, starting from base of the hole.
3 Spread the remaining *pale orange* buttercream over the rest of the cake and swirl with a knife.

TO MAKE THE HEAD

1 Mould the *yellow* sugarpaste into *two* sausage shapes about 45cm/18in long. Roll out flat to about 2cm/¾in wide; taper the ends.
2 Supporting one strip over your hand, place one end halfway along the back of the dinosaur on top of the hole, and guide the strip round the hole, down the front of the dinosaur and along the base of the cake to represent the under-side of the neck and belly. Position the second strip on other side of the dinosaur in the same way.
3 Roll out about half of the *orange* sugarpaste thickly. Using template Y, cut out *two* head pieces; place in position (see illustration 3).

Shaping Brontosaurus

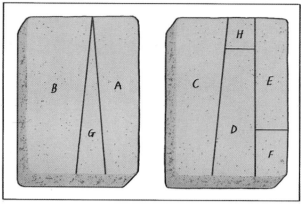

1 *Cut the two cakes, then slice horizontally through H to make two pieces.*

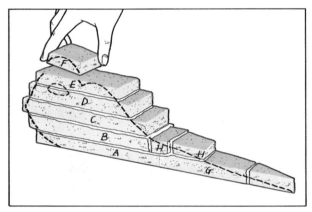

2 *Stack the cakes, then trim to shape. Using template Z, cut a hole to make the neck.*

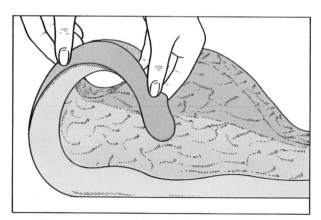

3 *Place an orange head piece on either side of the cake, above the yellow strip.*

TO MAKE THE FEET

1 Roll out remaining *orange* sugarpaste thickly. Using templates W and X, cut out the legs and press into position, allowing W to overlap X.

2 Mould the reserved *yellow* sugarpaste into toe nails and press into position.

TO FINISH THE CAKE

1 Use the *orange* colouring and a fine brush to outline the neck and head.

2 Use the *black* colouring to paint on the face features.

3 Press the mimosa balls over the top half of the dinosaur to decorate.

TEMPLATE FOR BRONTOSAURUS

HOLE Z

LEG X

LEG W

HEAD AND NECK Y

•PARASAUROLOPHUS•

par-a-*sawr*-oh-*loaf*-us

This duck-billed dinosaur had an extraordinary bone crest on top of its head. The crest contained breathing tubes and if the Parasaurolophus breathed out strongly it may have made a honking noise.

SERVES 15-20
LENGTH: 45cm/18in

CAKE

1 rectangular cake (see page 5)

ICING

250g/8oz buttercream (see page 10)
1kg/2lb quick sugarpaste (see page 10)

FOOD COLOURING

blue and *mauve* paste food colouring

TO SHAPE THE CAKE

1 Slice horizontally through the cake, then sandwich back together again with buttercream.
2 Make templates A, B, C, D, E and F (see page 43) and place on the cake as shown. Using a sharp knife, cut round the templates.
3 Arrange the body, tail and head (A, B and C) on the board and stick together with buttercream (see illustration, right).
4 Slice horizontally through the leg piece D and use one layer for the leg. Cut out another foot (E) from the spare leg piece and sandwich the two feet pieces together. Set leg, foot and crest aside.

TO COLOUR THE ICING

1 Reserve 30g/1oz *white* sugarpaste for claws.
2 Colour 125g/4oz sugarpaste *blue*.

3 Colour 185g/6oz sugarpaste *dark mauve*. Reserve 60g/2oz and knead the rest into the remaining sugarpaste to make *pale mauve*.

TO COVER THE CAKE

1 Spread a thin layer of buttercream over the body, head and tail.
2 Reserve 250g/8oz *pale mauve* sugarpaste and roll out the remainder to a strip about 43 × 20cm/ 17 × 8in, tapering each end.
3 Lay the sugarpaste strip over cake and gently ease it round the head and body and down the tail.
4 Smooth over the sugarpaste, trim and push the

Assembling The Cake

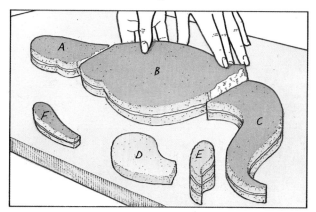

Stick the body, head and tail together. Make extra height for the foot from a layer of D.

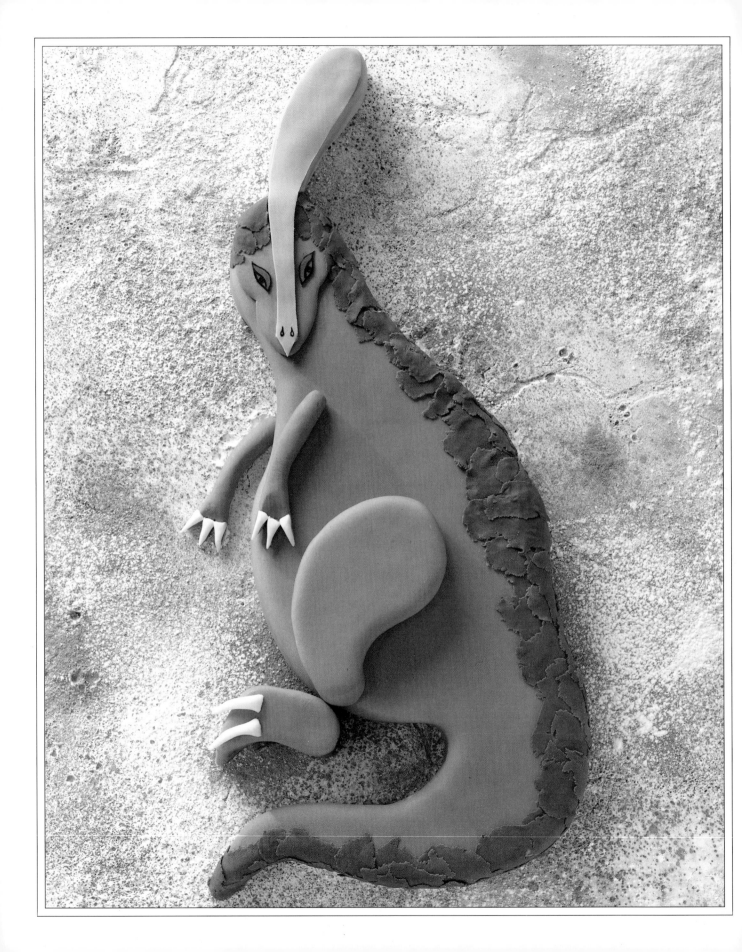

excess under to neaten.

5 Roll out a small piece of the reserved *pale mauve* sugarpaste. Using part of template A, cut out the face and place in position.

TO MAKE THE LEG AND ARMS

1 Lightly spread buttercream over the leg and foot.

2 Mould two small pieces of *pale mauve* sugarpaste into arms, place in position and cut the ends into fingers.

3 Roll out remaining *pale mauve* sugarpaste and cover the leg and foot using about half for each piece. Neaten and place in position, moistening at the ankle to seal, if necessary.

TO FINISH THE CAKE

1 Roll out the *dark mauve* sugarpaste very thinly and tear into small ragged pieces. Moisten the back and tail and press on the torn pieces, overlapping them slightly.

2 Cut two *dark mauve* sugarpaste eyes.

3 Lightly spread the cake crest piece (F) with buttercream. Roll out the *blue* sugarpaste. Using template G, cut out the long crest piece; reserve. Cover cake crest piece with remaining *blue* sugarpaste and place at top of head.

4 Ease sugarpaste crest (G) onto face; place along nose to end of cake. Mould to shape.

5 Mould the *white* sugarpaste into nails.

6 Stick on eyes and paint face details.

TEMPLATE FOR PARASAUROLOPHUS

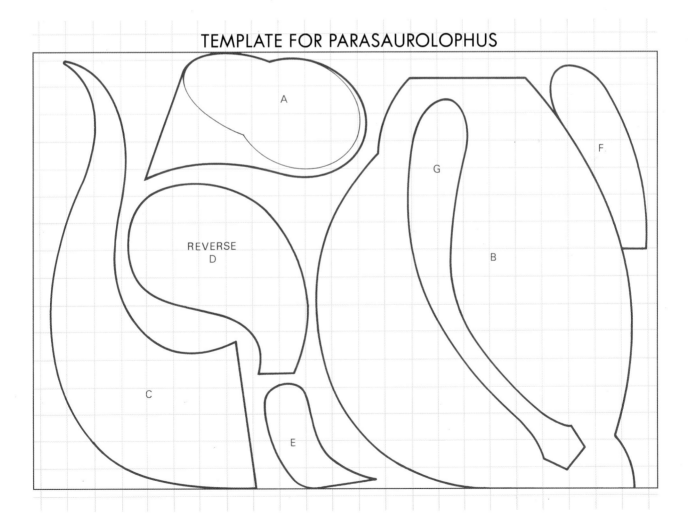

·STEGOSAURUS·

steg-oh-saw-rus

The Stegosaurus is easily recognized by the double row of bony plates running down its back. As a defence against meat-eaters, the Stegosaurus had two pairs of long curved bony spikes at the end of its tail which could be swung with deadly effect.

SERVES 20-25
LENGTH: 45cm/18in

The back plates should be made at least 24 hours in advance to allow them to set hard. Use rectangular, single-layered wafers for this recipe – these are widely available from supermarkets.

CAKES

1 rectangular cake (see page 5)
1 round 23cm/9in cake (see page 5)

ICING

2.5kg/5lb quick sugarpaste (see page 10)
750g/1½lb buttercream (see page 10)

FOOD COLOURING

pink, red, green, blue, yellow and *black* paste food colouring

DECORATION

20-25 ice cream wafers

TO COLOUR THE ICING

1 Colour 250g/8oz sugarpaste *pink*.
2 Colour 250g/8oz sugarpaste *red*.
3 Colour 1.75kg/3½lb sugarpaste *green*.
4 Colour 185g/6oz sugarpaste *blue*.
5 Colour 60g/2oz sugarpaste *yellow*.

TO MAKE THE BACK PLATES

1 Make templates 1, 2, 3, 4 and 5 (see page 47). Using a small sharp pointed knife, cut the wafers into the following:
two plates using template 1;
four plates using template 2;
six plates using template 3;
ten plates using template 4;
four plates using template 5.
2 Dust the surface lightly with cornflour (cornstarch) and roll out the *pink* sugarpaste, large enough to fit on all the wafer plates.
3 Lightly brush the rolled-out sugarpaste with water and lay the wafer plates on top. Lightly brush the wafers with water.
4 Roll out the *red* sugarpaste thinly and lay it over the wafers. Smooth the sugarpaste down between each plate to seal.
5 Cut carefully round each wafer, leaving a small margin of sugarpaste. Reverse half the plates and leave to dry on non-stick paper which has been lightly dusted with cornflour (cornstarch). Reserve the trimmings.

TO SHAPE THE BODY

1 Cut a 20cm/8in circle from one end of the rectangular cake and cut the rest of the cake into tail pieces (see illustration 1, page 46). Cut both round cakes in half.

Shaping And Assembling Stegosaurus

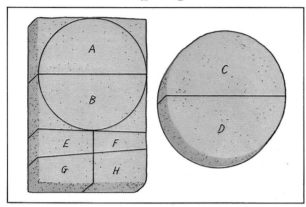

1 Cut a 20cm/8in circle from the rectangular cake; cut the rest into pieces.

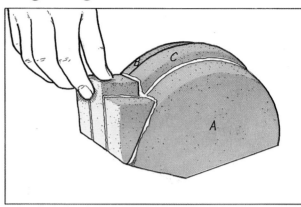

2 Cut a piece from one end of body, slide upwards and stick to make the front.

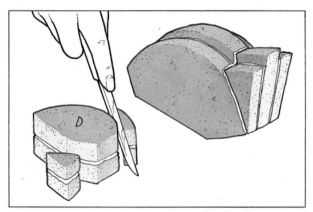

3 Cut away a small piece at the back. Cut piece D in half, stick together, then trim.

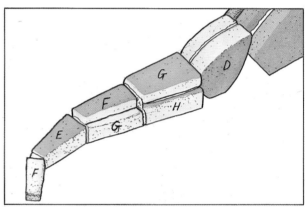

4 Place D at the back and assemble tail; cut out triangles to curve tail.

2 Sandwich ree semi-circles (A, B and C) together with buttercream, placing piece C in the middle, to make the body of the dinosaur. Place on the board.

3 Cut a small triangular shape from one end of the cake, then slide it upwards and stick in place at the beginning of the curve (see illustration 2). This will be the front of the dinosaur.

4 Cut a small triangular shape from the back of the cake. Cut the base of the cake slightly inwards and away from the board. Trim off the sharp edges along the top to make a smooth curved back to the dinosaur.

TO SHAPE THE TAIL

1 Cut the remaining semi-circle (D) in half, sandwich together with buttercream and trim off the corners (see illustration 3). Place in position but do not stick (see illustration 4).

2 Slice horizontally through the remaining cake pieces F and G, making the top layers thicker than the bottom layers. Stick all the remaining pieces in position at the tail end (see illustration 4).

3 Trim and shape the tail. Cut the base of the tail inwards away from the board and curve the tail forwards (see illustration 4).

TEMPLATE FOR STEGOSAURUS

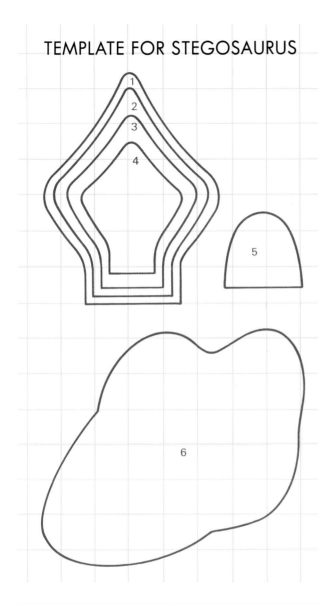

1
2
3
4
5
6

TO POSITION THE PLATES

1 Reserve about 15g/½oz *blue* sugarpaste and roll the remainder into a long sausage shape the length of the dinosaur, thick at one end and tapering down to a point at the other end. Flatten the roll slightly.

2 Moisten the backbone and top of the tail and place the flattened roll along the length of the back and tail. With your fingers, gently spread the edges outwards to form an irregular shape. Leave the middle of the flattened roll as thick as possible to form a good base for the plates.

3 With a pointed knife, make two deep slits along the back of the body between the cakes. Make one long cut down the length of the tail.

4 Gently push the plates into the slits, pushing up the *blue* sugarpaste slightly to support them. Lightly moisten the sugarpaste, if necessary, and ensure all the plates face the correct way.

5 If the plates begin to flop, support them with pieces of crumpled kitchen paper and remove the paper just before serving.

6 Break off tiny pieces of the reserved *blue* sugarpaste and smooth onto the top half of the body in an irregular pattern. If the pieces do not stick in place, dampen lightly with the tip of a paint brush before smoothing into position.

TO COVER THE CAKE

1 Separate the tail from the body. Measure the length and breadth of the body and then the tail.

2 Spread the body and tail with buttercream.

3 Roll out 1kg/2lb *green* sugarpaste to cover the body and smooth over.

4 Roll out 375g/12oz *green* sugarpaste to cover the tail. Carefully push the tail back into position and smooth over the join to neaten.

5 Trim the sugarpaste and push under the tail and body to neaten. Prick all over the body and tail with a cocktail stick.

TO FINISH THE CAKE

1 Roll out the remaining *green* sugarpaste thickly. Using template 6, cut out one head. Re-roll the trimmings and, using templates 7 and 8 (see page 11), cut out front and back legs.

2 Stick the head and legs in position and smooth off the sharp edges by rubbing gently with fingers dusted with icing (confectioner's) sugar or cornflour (cornstarch).

3 Mould the *yellow* sugarpaste into a beak for the nose and four spikes for the end of the tail. Stick in place.

4 Mould the reserved *red* and *pink* trimmings into claws and stick onto the feet.

5 Use *black* colouring and a thin brush to paint on the eyes and nostrils.

◆ TYRANNOSAURUS REX ◆

tie-*ran*-oh-*saw*-rus rex

This fierce meat-eater was one of the largest dinosaurs, measuring up to 5m/16ft high when it stood upright. It had powerful back legs, a short stout body and an enormous head with strong jaws capable of consuming large chunks of flesh.

SERVES 25-30
LENGTH: 45cm/18in

CAKES

1 pudding bowl cake, made in a
1.57 litre/50fl oz/6 cup bowl (see page 6)
1 rectangular Madeira cake (see page 6)

ICING

500g/1lb buttercream (see page 10)
2kg/4lb quick sugarpaste (see page 10)

FOOD COLOURING

pink paste food colouring
brown, *pink*, *green* and *yellow* paste, liquid or
powder food colouring

TO SHAPE THE CAKE

1 Slice horizontally through pudding bowl cake three times to make four layers. Sandwich back together with buttercream and place on board.
2 Slice through the rectangular cake to make two layers. Using template X (see page 51), cut out two heads from one layer. Cut out one head and tail pieces from the second layer (see illustration 1, page 50).
3 Trim the pudding bowl cake back and front and at a slight angle down towards the tail. Cut the base of the cake inwards away from the board.
4 Use the cake trimmings to make a backbone.

5 Assemble the tail pieces at the back and stick together with buttercream. Trim and curve the tail (see illustration 2).
6 Sandwich two head pieces together with buttercream.

TO COLOUR THE ICING

1 Colour 250g/8oz sugarpaste dark *pink*. Leave the remaining sugarpaste *white* and reserve 30g/1oz in plastic wrap for the teeth.

TO COVER THE CAKE

1 Spread a thin layer of buttercream over the body and tail.
2 Roll out 625g/1¼lb *white* sugarpaste to a 30cm/12in circle. Mark the sugarpaste by pressing the small holes of a grater firmly over the surface. Smooth it over the body. Trim base.
3 Roll out 250g/8oz *white* sugarpaste into a strip at least 40cm/16in long and 15cm/6in wide at the top. Mark with the grater. Ease the strip along the length of the tail, making small pleats where necessary. Smooth over the join with the body. Push the excess sugarpaste under to neaten and carefully lift up the end of the tail.
4 Roll out 60g/2oz *white* sugarpaste and using template Y, cut out the back leg. Mould the front arm using 30g/1oz *white* sugarpaste. Mark arm and leg with the grater and stick in position.

Shaping And Assembling Tyrannosaurus Rex

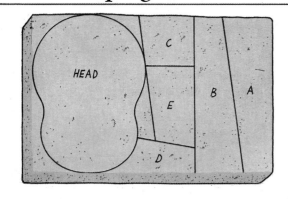

1 From the second layer of cake, cut out a head and the tail pieces.

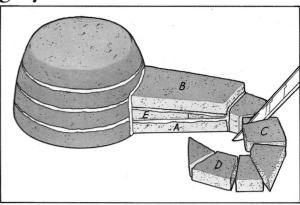

2 Stick the tail pieces in position. Curve the tail by cutting out triangular pieces.

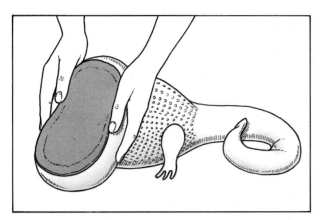

3 Stick the thickest head piece onto the body and hold firmly in place for a few minutes.

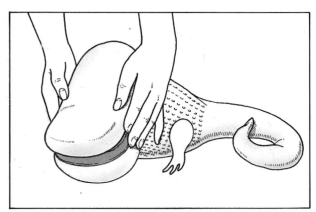

4 Position second head piece, so that the inside of the mouth is revealed.

TO MAKE THE HEAD

1 Roll out 750g/1½lb *white* sugarpaste. Using template X, cut out two heads with at least 5cm/2in margin all round. Mould the trimmings into two small balls for the eyes and a small thin roll for the nasal structure. Stick in position on the thinner cake head piece.

2 Spread the top and sides of each head-shaped cake with buttercream and lay a piece of head-shaped sugarpaste on top of each. Smooth over and work down the sides.

3 Turn the cakes over and lay them on non-stick paper. Spread a little buttercream on top and draw the excess sugarpaste on to the top. Press down well. Leave the cakes in place on the non-stick paper.

4 Roll out the *pink* sugarpaste. Using template X, cut out two heads. Place the *pink* pieces on top of the cakes, positioning them slightly forward at the mouth end in order to make the gums. Press and smooth the edges of the *pink* and *white* sugarpaste together.

5 Turn the cakes over and smooth round eyes and nose. Mark the sugarpaste with the grater.

TO POSITION THE HEAD

1 *Use buttercream to stick the thickest head piece, *pink* side uppermost, on to the end of the body (see illustration 3). Hold for a few minutes.

2 Spread back half with buttercream and place the second head piece, *white* side uppermost, on top, positioning it so that the back edge hangs slightly over the back of the head, revealing the inside of the lower jaw (see illustration 4).

3 Press the cake firmly in position and hold for a few seconds. Smooth the join round the back of the head first with a knife and then with fingers.

*Alternatively, assemble the head separately and leave to set before placing on body.

TO FINISH THE CAKE

1 Roll out reserved 30g/1oz *white* sugarpaste into two narrow strips about 23cm/9in long. Cut out small triangular shapes along one edge of each strip to make teeth; keep each strip in one piece. Moisten the mouth edges and press the strips of teeth into position.

2 Using a clean pastry brush, brush *brown* colouring in a swirling pattern over the surface of the dinosaur, leaving a few areas to brush *yellow* and *green*.

3 Colour the *white* sugarpaste trimmings *green* and use to mould claws. Stick in position. Use *brown* colouring to paint on eyes and nostrils.

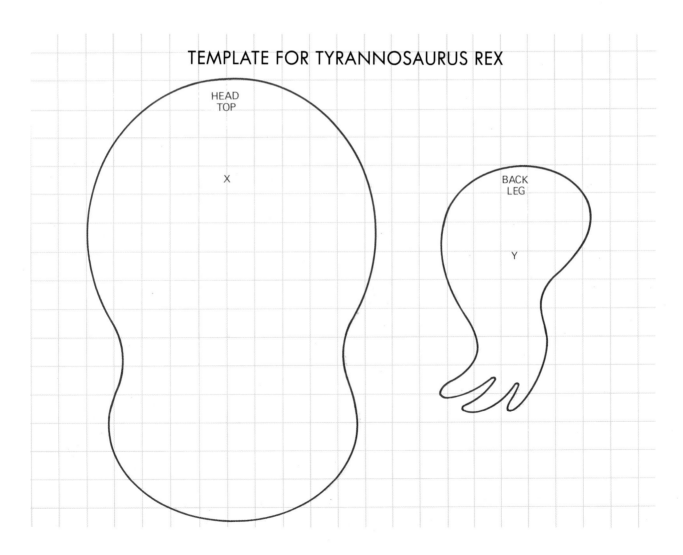

TEMPLATE FOR TYRANNOSAURUS REX

HEAD
TOP

X

BACK
LEG

Y

·PTERANODON·

ter-*an*-oh-*don*

This flying prehistoric reptile had a wing span of up to 7m/23ft which enabled it to swoop down over the sea and scoop up fish with its long beak. It may even have had a pouch beneath its beak for storing fish.

SERVES 15-20
LENGTH: 33cm/13in

After a few hours the rice paper wings will begin to curl giving an effect of movement.

CAKE

1 rectangular Madeira cake (see page 6)

ICING

250g/8oz buttercream (see page 10)
750g/1½lb quick sugarpaste (see page 10)

FOOD COLOURING

blue, pink, yellow, orange and *mauve* powder food colouring

DECORATION

rice paper, measuring 45 × 15cm/18 × 6in (see page 11)

TO SHAPE THE CAKE

1 Slice horizontally through the cake, then sandwich together with buttercream.
2 Spread a layer of buttercream all over the cake.

TO COLOUR THE ICING

1 Lightly knead a little *blue* colouring into the sugarpaste to make a streaky *pale blue*.

2 Divide off 125g/4oz sugarpaste and continue adding *blue* colouring to this quantity until an even *dark blue*.

TO COVER THE CAKE

1 Roll out the streaky *pale blue* sugarpaste into a rectangle about 40 × 30cm/16 × 12in.
2 Lay the sugarpaste over the cake, smoothing it over the top and allowing the excess to fall loosely down the sides, onto the board.
3 Trim sugarpaste leaving a 1cm/½in margin on the board (see illustration 1, page 54).
4 Using a dry brush, lightly brush the powder colouring across the cake to create a sunset scene.

TO MAKE THE WINGS

1 Brush *blue* colouring over the rice paper.
2 Using template A (see page 54), cut out rice paper wings with sharp scissors. Cut out as one piece, or as two, if the paper is not large enough. Lightly place wings on the cake – *do not stick.*

TO FINISH THE CAKE

1 Roll out the *dark blue* sugarpaste thickly. Using template B, cut out the head and body and place in position on the wings.
2 Using trimmings, roll out two long thin strips for arms and two shorter strips for legs. Stick in position (see illustration 2). Paint on the eye.

Shaping And Assembling Pteranodon

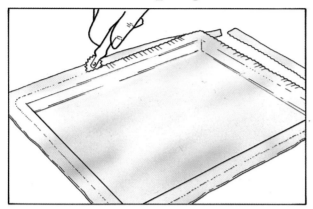

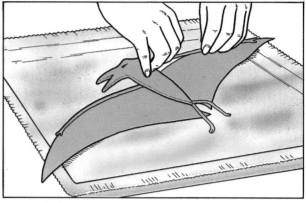

1 *Cut off the excess sugarpaste with a pastry wheel, leaving a 1cm/½in border.*

2 *Lightly place the wings on the cake, then press the body, arms and legs in position.*

TEMPLATE FOR PTERANODON

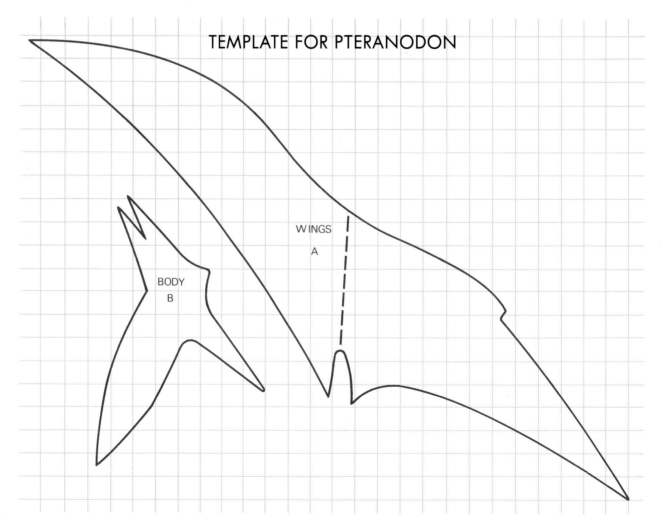

WINGS
A

BODY
B

·CHASMOSAURUS·

kaz-mo-*saw*-rus

Looking very like the rhinoceros of today, the plant-eating Chasmosaurus was extremely sturdy and well armed, with three large horns on its head. A distinctive bony frill covered its neck.

SERVES 20-25
LENGTH: 45cm/18in

CAKE

3 round 20cm/8in cakes (see page 5)

ICING

1kg/2lb buttercream (see page 10)
250g/8oz quick sugarpaste (see page 10)

FOOD COLOURING

blue, *yellow* and *green* paste
food colouring

DECORATION

3 ice cream wafer cones
125g/4oz round liquorice sweets

TO SHAPE THE CAKE

1 Sandwich the three cakes together with buttercream, pressing them firmly into position.
2 Measure 5cm/2in in from the edge of the cake and cut off piece B.
3 Cut away pieces C and D and cut the head from piece B (see illustration 1, page 57).
4 Stand the body piece A on the board. Remove one layer from head to use for the tail. Stick the head onto the body with buttercream and hold for a few minutes (see illustration 2). Support the nose with an egg cup until set.

5 Split up the cake layers of pieces C and D and use to make the legs and part of the tail (see illustration 3). Stick in position.
6 Stick the reserved layer of piece B onto the end of the tail (see illustration 3).
7 Cover the cake with foil and leave to set for several hours or overnight.

TO COLOUR THE ICING

1 Colour 125g/4oz sugarpaste *blue*.
2 Colour 125g/4oz sugarpaste *yellow*.
3 Remove 3 rounded tablespoons buttercream and colour *yellow*. Add a little *green* colouring to the remaining buttercream to make a bright shade.

TO MAKE THE HORNS

1 Cover the pointed tips of the ice cream cones with *yellow* sugarpaste (see page 13). Leave to dry.
2 Cut diagonally across the wide ends of the cones so that two horns measure 5cm/2in on the shortest side, and one measures 3.5cm/1½in on the shortest side (see page 13).
3 Reserve *yellow* trimmings for spikes and eyes.

TO COVER THE CAKE

1 Spread the *yellow* buttercream over the underbelly of the dinosaur and smooth over.
2 Cover all the other parts of the cake with *green*

Shaping And Assembling Chasmosaurus

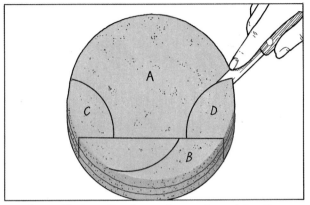

1 Cut off piece B, then pieces C and D. Cut a head shape from B.

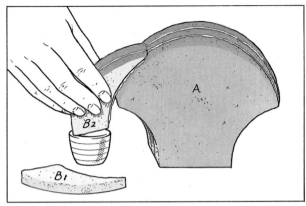

2 Remove one layer from the head for the tail (B1). Stick head in place.

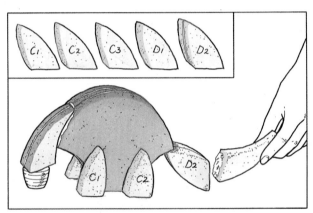

3 Split up C and D to make legs and beginning of tail. Add reserved B1.

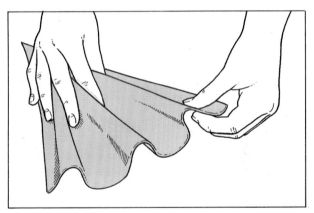

4 To make the frill, roll under the sides and pleat the base edge into three soft folds.

---

buttercream, not forgetting under the nose. The egg cup must be replaced afterwards: remove just before serving.

3 Smooth the *green* buttercream with a knife along the body, legs and tail.

TO MAKE THE FRILL

1 Roll out the *blue* sugarpaste thickly into a triangle with 20cm/8in sides. Roll under the two side edges and pleat the base (see illustration 4).

2 Place the frill on top of the dinosaur's head, gently moulding the pleated edge around the neck. As the frill dries, lift up the tip end carefully so that it does not lie flat against the back.

3 Mould twelve spikes from remaining *yellow* sugarpaste and position on frill.

TO FINISH THE CAKE

1 Place the shortest horn on the nose and the remaining two on the dinosaur's brow.

2 Mould remaining *yellow* sugarpaste into teardrop-shaped eyes. Paint on pupils.

3 Arrange the liquorice sweets down the length of dinosaur. Use two half buttons for nostrils.

·ICHTHYOSTEGA·

ik-*thee*-oh-*steg*-a

*Ichthyostega was the earliest known land animal,
although it still had strong amphibian features, such as
a scaley skin. The strong backbone and ribs enabled it
to support itself on land.*

SERVES 15-20
LENGTH: 50cm/20in

CAKES

1 rectangular cake (see page 5)

ICING

375g/12oz buttercream (see page 10)
750g/1½lb quick sugarpaste (see page 10)

FOOD COLOURING

yellow, mauve and *black* paste food colouring
pink and *blue* powder or paste
food colouring

TO SHAPE THE CAKE

1 Slice horizontally through the cake and sandwich back together with buttercream.
2 Make templates A, B, C, D and E (see page 60) and place on the cake as shown. Using a sharp knife, cut round the templates.
3 Sandwich the two main body pieces (A) together with buttercream. Press the layers together firmly and leave to set before standing the cake on the board (see illustration, right).
4 Stick the tail in place (see illustration).
5 Trim off the sharp edges along the back, then stick the trimmings on top to make a backbone. Trim the cake at a sharp angle at the front to make the nose.
6 Cut the cake inwards at the base.

TO COLOUR THE ICING

1 Colour 60g/2oz sugarpaste bright *yellow*.
2 Colour the remaining sugarpaste pale *mauve*.

TO COVER THE CAKE

1 Spread a thin layer of buttercream over cake.
2 Reserve 125g/4oz *mauve* sugarpaste for feet and roll remainder into a piece 50cm/20in long and 25cm/10in wide at one end, tapering down at the other end to make the tail.
3 Lay over the cake and smooth over the body and tail, and round the nose. Push the excess under.

Assembling Ichthyostega

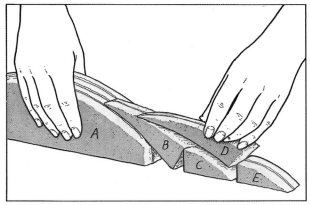

*Sandwich the body pieces together, then
assemble the tail. Fill gaps with buttercream.*

TEMPLATE FOR ICHTHYOSTEGA

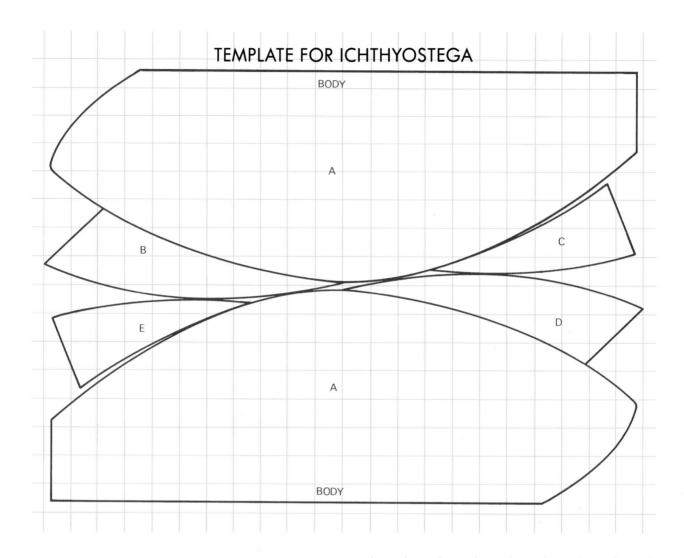

BODY

A

B

C

E

D

A

BODY

TO FINISH THE CAKE

1 Mould 45g/1½oz *yellow* sugarpaste into a 23cm/9in sausage; taper each end into a point.

2 Stick the *yellow* strip on top of the tail.

3 Lightly smear *yellow* colouring on the underside of the cake, or brush on powder.

4 Roll out the reserved *mauve* sugarpaste thickly. Using templates X and Y, cut out four legs and stick them in position, with feet flat on the board.

5 Smear or brush small patches of *pink* and *blue* colouring over the body and legs.

6 Use remaining *yellow* sugarpaste to make claws and torn pieces for the back (see page 43).

7 Paint *black* horizontal stripes along the *yellow* strip on the tail. Paint on the eyes and mouth.

TEMPLATE FOR ICHTHYOSTEGA

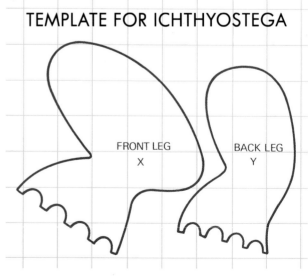

FRONT LEG
X

BACK LEG
Y

·BRACHIOSAURUS·

brack-ee-oh-*saw*-rus

*This huge plant-eating dinosaur grew up to a length of
25m/82ft and had an extremely long neck that could
stretch up to a great height. It was able to eat from the
tops of trees, beyond the reach of other plant-eaters.*

SERVES 15-20
LENGTH: 50cm/20in

CAKE

1 rectangular cake (see page 5)

ICING

500g/1lb buttercream (see page 10)

FOOD COLOURING

green and *blue* paste or liquid food colouring

DECORATION

small *pink* jelly sweets

TO SHAPE THE CAKE

1 Slice horizontally through the cake, then sandwich back together again with buttercream.
2 Make templates A, B, C, D and E (see page 63).
Place on the cake as shown. Using a sharp knife,
cut round the templates.
3 Arrange the cake pieces on the board; stick
with buttercream (see illustration, right).
4 Spread a thin layer of buttercream over the top
and sides of the cake.

TO COLOUR THE ICING

1 Colour 1 rounded tablespoon buttercream
green. Colour the remainder *blue*.

TO COVER THE CAKE

1 Spread the top and sides of the assembled cake
with *blue* buttercream and swirl with a knife.
2 Using a small round-bladed knife, swirl the
green buttercream over the *blue* icing.

TO FINISH THE CAKE

1 Cut the jelly sweets into toe nail shapes and
place in position. Press one jelly sweet next to the
mouth for the tongue, if wished.
2 Dip a skewer into the *green* colouring and use
to mark on the eye and mouth.

Assembling Brachiosaurus

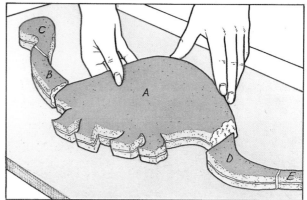

*Position the cake pieces on the board to make
the shape of the dinosaur. Stick in place.*

TEMPLATE FOR BRACHIOSAURUS

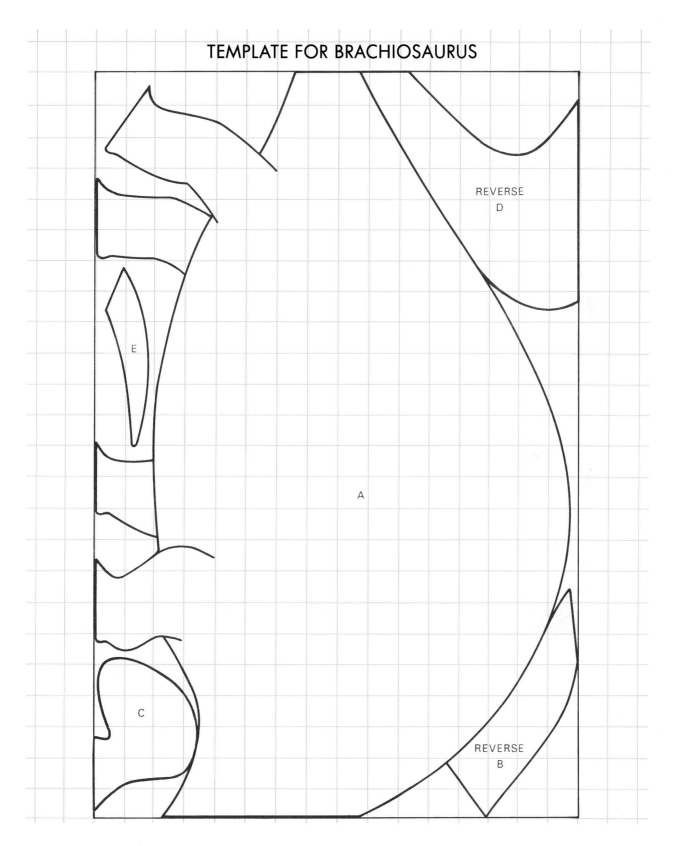

REVERSE
D

E

A

C

REVERSE
B

·SCELIDOSAURUS·

s k e l - *i d e* - o h - *s a w* - r u s

The plant-eating Scelidosaurus had a bony armour plating which was formed into ridges for easy movement. The plating was covered in bony spikes and knobs, providing excellent protection against predators

SERVES 20-25
LENGTH: 48cm/19in

Do not make up the chocolate fudge icing until you need to use it.

CAKES

1 Swiss roll sponge, tightly rolled widthwise (see page 7)
1 Swiss roll sponge, loosely rolled lengthwise (see page 7)
1 round 20cm/8in sponge, (see page 5)

ICING

2 × basic quantity chocolate fudge icing (see page 9)
about 3 tablespoons jam, warmed and sieved
1.25kg/2½lb white marzipan

FOOD COLOURING

pink, *yellow* and *black* paste food colouring

DECORATIONS

small wine gums or jellies

TO SHAPE THE CAKE

1 Make up 1 quantity chocolate fudge icing for assembling the cake.
2 Gently unroll the widthwise-rolled sponge. Spread with the fudge icing, re-roll and place on the cakeboard with the join underneath.
3 Unroll the second sponge, spread with fudge icing and lay over the first sponge, making it flush at one end so that the excess sponge hangs down at the other end. Mould the overhanging sponge to form the beginning of the tail (see illustration 1, page 66).
4 Using template X (see page 67), cut out the head from the round sponge and cut the remaining cake into pieces (see illustration 2).
5 Assemble the tail and stick in place with icing (see illustration 3).
6 Spread the remaining pieces of cake with buttercream or jam and arrange on the board. Carefully lift the dinosaur and place on top of the cake pieces to raise the body off the board.
7 Cover the cake with foil and leave to set for at least 30 minutes.

TO COLOUR THE ICING

1 Colour 560g/1lb 2oz marzipan *pale pink*.
2 Colour 560g/1lb 2oz marzipan *dark pink*.
3 Colour 125g/4oz marzipan *yellow*.
4 Wrap the marzipan until ready to use.

TO COVER THE CAKE

1 Make up 1 quantity fudge icing and spread thinly over the body and tail of the dinosaur. Spread icing over the head, reserving a small amount for the mouth.

Shaping And Assembling Scelidosaurus

1 Mould the overhanging sponge to form the beginning of the tail.

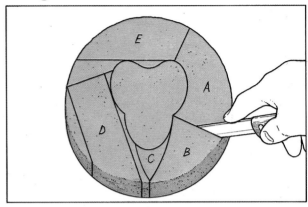

2 Cut out the head from the round sponge; cut the rest into pieces.

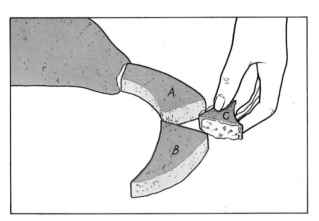

3 Assemble the tail pieces at the moulded end of the body and stick in place.

4 Cut a 7.5cm/3in slit to make the mouth. Shape the marzipan inner mouth piece.

2 Roll out the *pale pink* marzipan to a strip 45cm/18in long and 20cm/8in wide at one end, tapering down to about 7.5cm/3in at other end.

3 Lay the marzipan over the cake and smooth down, pushing the excess under the cake, to neaten.

4 Reserve 250g/8oz *dark pink* marzipan for the head and roll out the remainder into a strip about 20cm/8in wide. Cut strips about 3.5cm/1½in wide across the width and stick onto the body with jam; leave a 3.5cm/1½in space between each strip. Trim the strips at the base, to neaten, and smooth along the edges of each strip to blend into the main marzipan. Use slightly narrower strips towards the tip of the tail.

TO MAKE THE HEAD

1 Roll out the reserved *dark pink* marzipan to a 25cm/10in circle.

2 Using template X, cut out the head shape, allowing a 5cm/2in margin all round. Mould two small balls from the trimmings, flatten slightly and stick in the eye positions on the cake.

3 Place the marzipan over the head and smooth it down the sides. Invert the covered head onto a

piece of greaseproof (waxed) paper.

4 Mould the excess marzipan over the back and stick with icing or jam. Turn the head over and smooth round the eyes.

5 Using a sharp knife, cut a 7.5cm/3in horizontal slit through the cake at the mouth end (see illustration 4). Gently open the mouth and spread with icing or jam.

6 Roll out 90g/3oz *yellow* marzipan to an oval shape about 15 × 7.5cm/6 × 3in.

7 Fold the piece in half and insert into the mouth slit. Prop the mouth open with two balls of marzipan and a row of sweets.

8 Pinch the edges of the *yellow* and *pink* marzipan firmly together to seal and make thick gums.

9 Leave the head to set before positioning.

TO FINISH THE CAKE

1 Knead the remaining *pink* marzipan trimmings together and roll out thickly. Using templates Y and Z, cut out two front and two back legs. Place in position on either side of the body, with the feet lying flat on the board.

2 Knead all the *yellow* marzipan trimmings together. Roll out a small quantity and cut out two small circles for the eyes. Stick in position.

3 Mould the remaining *yellow* marzipan into spikes and claws. Stick the spikes in a row along the back, taking care not to dent the marzipan covering the body. Position the claws on the feet.

4 Use *black* colouring to paint on the mouth, nose and eyes.

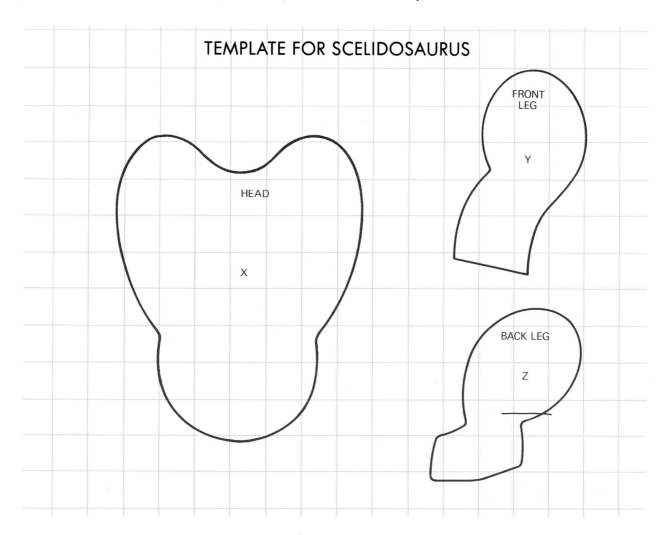

TEMPLATE FOR SCELIDOSAURUS

◆ DINOSAUR TABLEAU ◆

Styracosaurus, Brontosaurus, Stegosaurus and Dimetrodon are four of the better known prebistoric animals. All four have very distinctive features and as a group they look most impressive!

SERVES 15-20
LENGTH: 30cm/12in

You may like to add a Pteranodon to the tableau – paint onto the icing, using the templates on page 54 as a guide-line.

CAKES

1 rectangular Madeira cake (see page 6)

ICING

250g/8oz buttercream (see page 10)
1kg/2lb quick sugarpaste (see page 10)

FOOD COLOURING

black, brown, blue, green, yellow, red and *pink* paste or powder food colouring
black colouring pen (see page 8), optional

TO SHAPE THE CAKE

1 Slice horizontally through the cake and sandwich the layers together with buttercream.
2 Spread a thin layer of buttercream over the cake and down the sides.

TO COLOUR THE ICING

1 Reserve 185g/6oz sugarpaste for the cut-outs.
2 Cut the remaining piece into three thick slices and spread a skewer dipped in *black* colouring over the slices once only. Sandwich back together again.
3 Repeat the previous step, cutting in different places and using *brown* colouring.
4 Knead the sugarpaste very lightly until streaky. Do not overknead or the streaky effect will be lost.

TO COVER THE CAKE

1 Roll out the sugarpaste into a rectangle about 40 × 30cm/16 × 12in.
2 Lay the sugarpaste over the cake and let it fall loosely down the sides onto the board. Cut off the excess with a pastry wheel, leaving a margin of about 1cm/½in all round on the board.
3 Using a dry wide brush dipped in the coloured powders, lightly brush the colours across the cake to give the effect of grass, rocks, water, sand and so on, if wished.

TO MAKE THE DINOSAURS

1 Cut out templates of dinosaurs (see page 70).
2 Allow 45g/1½oz sugarpaste for each dinosaur, colouring 30g/1oz for each main body piece and the remainder for the other features. Cut out one dinosaur at a time so that the sugarpaste is still soft when positioned.
3 Roll out the sugarpaste on a surface lightly dusted with icing sugar to the thickness of pastry.
4 Place the template on the sugarpaste and cut round with a small knife, art knife or penknife. Remove the excess pieces, then carefully lift the shape with a round-bladed knife and place in position. If necessary, use cooled, boiled water or alcohol for sticking the shape in place, but make sure that the brush is only damp as excess liquid

TEMPLATE FOR DINOSAUR TABLEAU

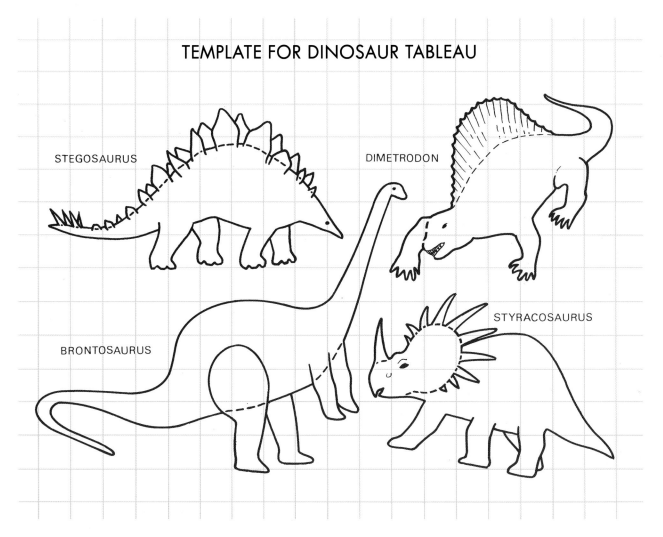

STEGOSAURUS

DIMETRODON

BRONTOSAURUS

STYRACOSAURUS

will dissolve the sugarpaste.

5 Round off the shape by gently rubbing the cut edges with a finger dipped lightly in icing sugar or cornflour.

6 Add the additional features and paint on the eyes.

Brontosaurus: colour all the sugarpaste for this dinosaur the same colour and cut out the main body, omitting the legs. Cut out four legs so that one back leg and one front leg overlap the body when placed in position.

Stegosaurus: cut out the body and legs in one piece, omitting the back plates. Using two colours, mould tiny pieces of sugarpaste into plates and place the back row of plates fat on the cake. Stick on the front row of plates so that they just touch

the back of the dinosaur. Add two white sugarpaste spikes to tail. Mark body with knife.

Dimetrodon: cut out the body and two legs in one piece, omitting one leg and the back fan. Cut out the back leg. Fill the mouth with white sugarpaste and paint on the teeth. Mark the body with the handle of the brush. Cut out the fan. Use the small end of a large plain piping nozzle to cut a scalloped edge round the fan and place on the cake. Paint on the black lines.

Styracosaurus: cut out the body, head and legs in one piece, omitting the horns. Mould the horns and arrange in position at the top of the head. Cut out another head and place over the original head and base of horns. Mark the body with the end of a pointed knife.

◆ DIMETRODON ◆

die-*mee*-tro-*don*

The extraordinary feature of this meat-eating reptile was the skin sail on top of its back. A row of tall, horny spines supported the sail which absorbed heat from the sun and warmed the blood.

SERVES 10-15
LENGTH: 30cm/12in

CAKES

1 ice cream sponge roll
1 Swiss roll sponge, loosely rolled lengthwise
(see page 7)

DECORATION

3 tablespoons jam, warmed
2 double fan wafer biscuits
8 ice cream wafer cones
500g/1lb white chocolate buttons

FOOD COLOURING

pink powder food colouring

TO SHAPE THE CAKE

1 Prepare the board and check freezer space.
2 Place ice cream roll on the board and brush with jam. Unwrap the Swiss roll sponge and lay it over the ice cream roll, so that the excess sponge hangs over at one end.
3 Mould the loose sponge to form the head (see illustration 1, page 73). Cover; return to freezer.

TO MAKE THE FIN

1 Using the wide end of an icing nozzle, cut out semi-circles from the outer edge of the wafer fans (see illustration 2).

2 Melt 75g/3oz chocolate buttons in a small bowl over a pan of hot water and colour dark *pink*. Either spread or brush the melted chocolate over one side of the fan wafers, using long strokes from the pointed end radiating outwards.
3 Place the wafers in the freezer until set, then turn them chocolate-side down onto non-stick paper. Cover the other sides with *pink* chocolate and return the fins to the freezer. Reserve the remaining *pink* chocolate.

TO MAKE THE TAIL AND FEET

1 Using a small sharp pointed knife, split two wafer cones in half lengthwise and trim off the pointed ends to form the feet (see illustration 3). Dip the feet into the reserved *pink* chocolate to coat well. Leave to set on non-stick paper. Reserve remaining *pink* chocolate.
2 Cut the tops off five cones, just below the last thick ridge (see illustration 4). These pieces will make up the tail.
3 Reserve four chocolate buttons and melt the remainder in a clean bowl over a pan of hot water.
4 Remove the cake from the freezer and assemble tail: dip the five cone tops into the *white* chocolate and place at end of cake to form the curve of the tail (see illustration 4). Dip both ends of the remaining whole cone into the chocolate; slot onto the tail. Dip two pointed cone ends into the chocolate and slot into each other to form the end of the tail (see illustration 4).

Shaping And Assembling Dimetrodon

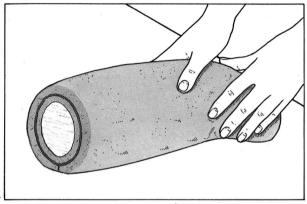

1 Mould the loose sponge to form the head; hold for a few minutes to set.

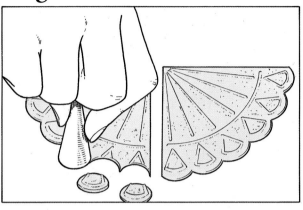

2 Using an icing nozzle, cut out semi-circles from the edge of the wafer.

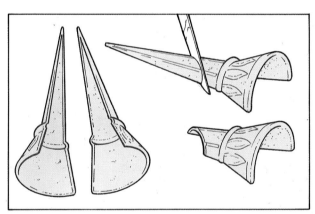

3 Split two cones and trim off the pointed ends to make the feet.

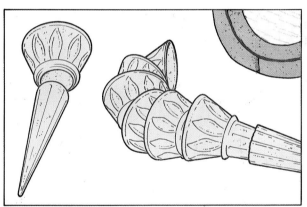

4 Cut the tops off five wafer cones; slot into each other to make the curved tail.

TO FINISH THE CAKE

1 Make an 18cm/7in slit along the centre back of the dinosaur and insert the two fins, sticking them into position with a little melted *white* chocolate.
2 Quickly spread the remaining *white* chocolate over the cake and tail, making a thick smooth snout on the head end. Place the feet in position and return the cake to the freezer.
3 Cut two chocolate buttons into slithers for the teeth and reserve. Re-melt the remaining *pink* chocolate.
4 Remove the cake from the freezer and use *pink* chocolate to seal the gap between the fins; to make the nose and mouth; to colour the end of the tail; to add spots to the body; and to stick and mark the teeth.
5 Use two chocolate buttons for the eyes, adding two *pink* spots to the centres. Return the cake to the freezer.

TO SERVE

Twenty minutes before serving, remove the cake from the freezer and place in the refrigerator to soften slightly.

·MOSASAURUS·

*mos-a-saw-*rus

The Mosasaurus had paddles for swimming, but used its long tail to speed through the water in order to catch large sea creatures or the flying reptiles that skimmed the surface of the sea.

SERVES 15-20
LENGTH: 53cm/21in

CAKES

1 rectangular cake (see page 5)

ICING

250g/8oz buttercream (see page 10)
Italian frosting, made with 2 eggs (see page 10)

FOOD COLOURING

blue powder food colouring
black paste or powder food colouring

DECORATION

rice paper (see page 11)
2 small jelly sweets

TO SHAPE THE CAKE

1 Make two templates each of A, B, C and D (see page 76) and place them on the cake as shown. Note that they are reversed on one side of cake. Using a sharp knife, cut round the templates.
2 Sandwich the matching body and tail pieces (A, B and C) together with butter cream, assemble on the board and cut the end to curve upwards (see illustration 1, page 76).
3 Stick the rock pieces (D) together with buttercream and reserve as a support for the head at a later stage (see illustration 1).

TO MAKE THE FINS AND FLIPPERS

1 Using a clean, dry pastry brush, evenly brush *blue* colouring over the rice paper. Repeat with the other side of the paper.
2 Cut out the following fins and flippers from the rice paper:
ten 2.5cm/1in square fins; ten 2cm/$\frac{3}{4}$in square fins; two flippers (see page 30).

TO COVER THE CAKE

1 Make up the Italian frosting and when stiff whisk in a little *blue* colouring to tint.
2 Carefully spread the frosting over the cake, starting at the front and supporting the head while you spread frosting under the chin. If you accidentally break the neck, use the rock to support the head (see illustration 2).

TO FINISH THE CAKE

1 Push the large paper squares into the soft icing at an angle, along the back of the dinosaur. Push the small paper squares along the tail and neck (see illustration 2).
2 Push the flippers into the sides of the cake so that they hang down onto the board.
3 Push the jelly sweets into the head for eyes.
4 Add a little *black* colouring to the leftover buttercream and spread this over the reserved piece of cake to make the rock.

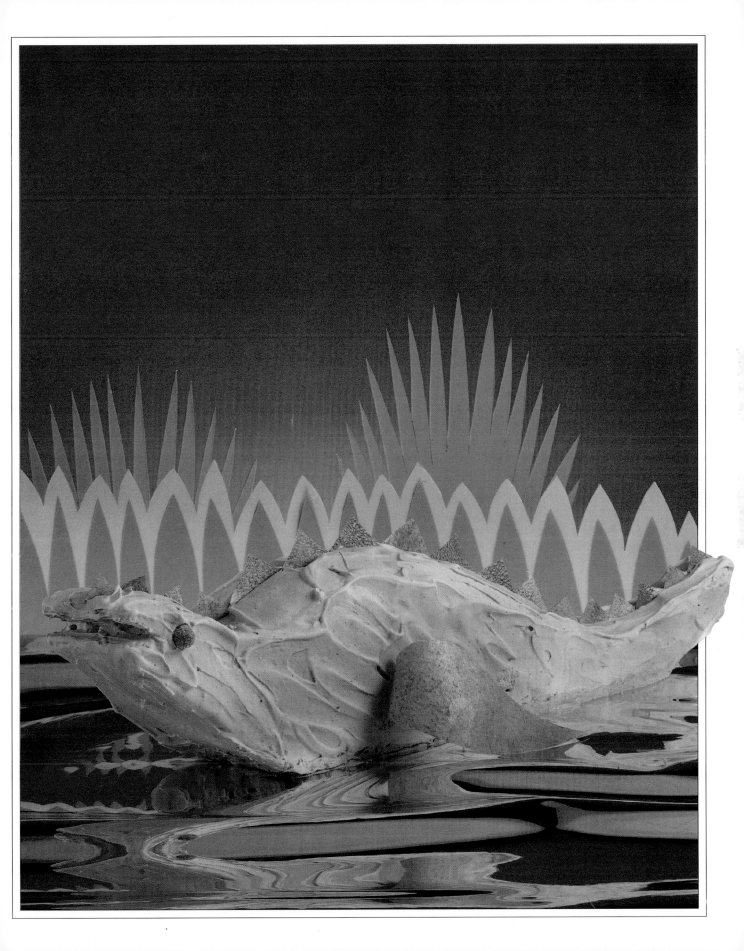

Shaping And Assembling Mosasaurus

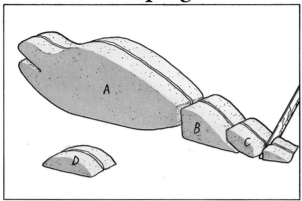

1 Assemble the cake and cut a triangular piece from C to curve tail.

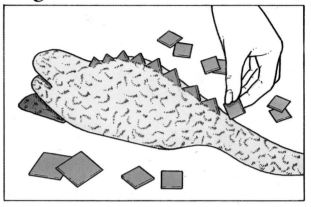

2 Position the larger squares along back and smaller squares along tail and neck.

TEMPLATE FOR MOSASAURUS

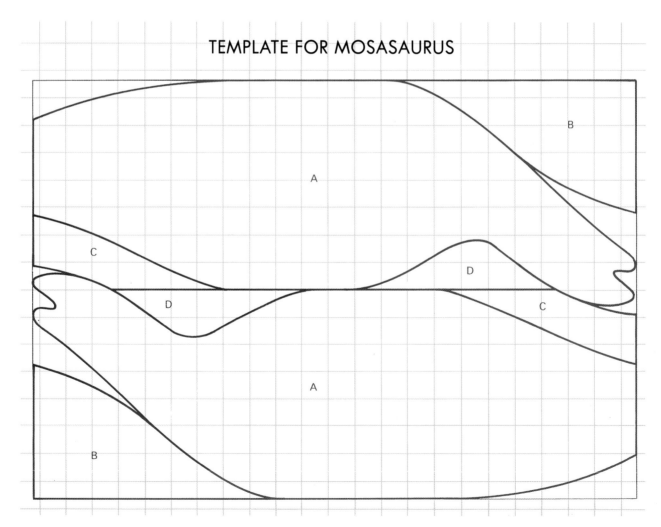

·TRICERATOPS·

try-*ser*-a-tops

The Triceratops was a peaceful plant-eater, but if it was attacked by a meat-eater it would swing its great horned head in a fearsome way. The large frill at the back of the Triceratop's head protected its neck from the sharp teeth of any assailant.

SERVES 20-25
HEIGHT: 36cm/14in

This cake reveals a delightful surprise when it is cut open.

CAKE

2 pudding bowl cakes, made in a 1.25litre/40fl oz/5 cup bowl (see page 6)

ICING

375g/12oz buttercream (see page 10)
1.5kg/3lb quick sugarpaste (see page 10)

FOOD COLOURING

blue and *pink* paste food colouring

EXTRAS

125g/4oz small sweets

TO SHAPE THE CAKE

1 Slice the top off the wide end of each cake and reserve for the head.
2 Slice horizontally through each cake twice. Using a 6cm/2½in cutter, cut out the centre of the two largest layers of each cake (see illustration 1, page 79). Reserve the cut out circles for the nose and feet.
3 Sandwich the layers of each cake back together with buttercream.
4 Wrap the sweets in plastic wrap and place inside the hollowed-out cakes (see illustration 2). Sandwich the two cakes together to make the body (see illustration 3). Leave the cake to set.
5 Trim down one side of the body cake to make a flat base. Place on the board.

TO COLOUR THE ICING

1 Colour 250g/8oz sugarpaste *blue*
2 Colour the remaining sugarpaste *pink*.

TO COVER THE CAKE

1 Spread buttercream over the body and head.
2 Roll out 625g/1¼lb *pink* sugarpaste into a 30cm/12in circle and smooth over the body. Trim and neaten. Prick all over with a straw.

TO MAKE THE HEAD

1 Sandwich the reserved head pieces together and cut to shape (see illustration 3). Stick a circle of cake on the narrow part to make a nose base.
2 Mould 30g/1oz *pink* sugarpaste into a hooked nose and place in position.
3 Roll out 375g/12oz *pink* sugarpaste into a 25cm/10in circle; smooth over head and nose.
4 Push the excess under the head; stick and trim and flatten as much as possible. Leave to set.

Shaping And Assembling Triceratops

1 Slice the cakes and cut out the centres of the two largest layers.

2 Sandwich the layers back together again and place sweets inside the hollows.

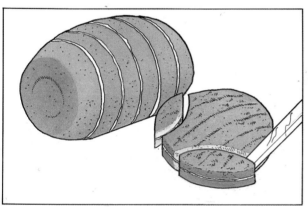

3 Sandwich the two cakes together to make the body. Stick and cut the head pieces.

4 Mould the sugarpaste over the back of the head; bring the scalloped edge onto the top.

TO MAKE THE TAIL AND FEET

1 Mould 60g/2oz *pink* sugarpaste into a thick tail about 10cm/4in long, tapering to a point at one end. Squash the thick end in to form a circle 6cm/2½in in diameter. Moisten the circle and stick the tail in position, smoothing out the join with a knife.

2 Cut one reserved cake circle into four feet. Roll out the remaining *pink* sugarpaste and cut out four 7.5cm/3in circles. Spread with buttercream and wrap round the feet, pushing the excess under. Stick the feet in position.

TO FINISH THE CAKE

1 Roll out the *blue* sugarpaste thickly and cut out a semi-circle with a base length of 20cm/8in to make the frill. Scallop the outer edge, moisten the surface and place the head on top, positioning it so that the scalloped edge can be brought right over the top of the head (see illustration 4).

2 Moisten the back of the frill and stick the head against the front of the body.

3 Mould the remaining *blue* sugarpaste into three horns and the claws. Stick in position.

6 Paint on the eyes and nostrils.

INDEX